Table of Contents

Pathway to Faith

Inspiring Stories from Catholic Saints,
Visionaries and Exorcists

by

Dr. ant

Copyright 2024 Dr. ant. All rights reserved.

No part of this book may be reproduced in any form or by any electronic or mechanical means including information storage and retrieval systems, without permission in writing from the author. The only exception is by a reviewer, who may quote short excerpts in a review.

Although the author and publisher have made every effort to ensure that the information in this book was correct at press time, the author and publisher do not assume and hereby disclaim any liability to any party for any loss, damage, or disruption caused by errors or omissions, whether such errors or omissions result from negligence, accident, or any other cause.

This publication is designed to provide accurate and authoritative information with regard to the subject matter covered. It is sold with the understanding that the publisher is not engaged in rendering professional services. If legal advice or other expert assistance is required, the services of a competent professional should be sought.

The fact that an organization or website is referred to in this work as a citation and/or a potential source of further information does not mean that the author or the publisher endorses the information the organization or website may provide or recommendations it may make.

Please remember that Internet websites listed in this work may have changed or disappeared between when this work was written and when it is read.

Pathway to Faith: Inspiring Stories from Catholic Saints, Visionaries and Exorcists

Contents

Contact Information for Prayer Groups and Support

Introduction

Welcome, fellow seekers of faith and truth. This book is not merely a collection of tales and anecdotes but a spiritual journey, carefully woven to enkindle the flame of faith and illuminate the path of righteousness. It is for those who believe, those who doubt, and even those who've strayed far into the wilderness of skepticism. Here, we will explore the depths of Roman Catholic spirituality and the timeless wisdom that has guided millions.

Understanding and embracing faith is not an easy task; it's nuanced, challenging, and, at times, terrifying. Yet, it is also joyful, uplifting, and filled with moments of divine clarity. Through the stories of saints, mystics, and ordinary believers, we aim to guide you through this divine tapestry. We have carefully selected each account to inspire, frighten, motivate, and even amuse you.

Imagine the life-transforming power of standing before a miracle. The saints' lives are filled with such awe-inspiring moments that defy logic and kindle a sense of divine wonder. These stories are more than history lessons; they are testaments to the strength and courage that faith can imbue in a person. For instance, when God transforms bread and wine into the Body and Blood during the Eucharist, it is not just a ritual; it is a divine miracle that has the power to change hearts and lives.

But faith is not only about the grand and miraculous. Equally powerful are the daily acts of kindness and the personal battles fought in quiet desperation. The lesser-known saints, like St. Josephine Bakhita and St. Andre Bessette, shine as beacons of humility and perseverance. Their lives remind us that greatness in God's eyes often lies in the most unseen corners of human experience.

Yet, the path to holiness isn't without its harrowing encounters. The mystics and visionaries like St. Catherine of Genoa and Blessed Anne Catherine Emmerich provide us with vivid glimpses into the spiritual warfare that surrounds us. Their experiences offer both consolation and a stark warning, reminding us of the ever-present battle between good and evil. Horror, in this context, isn't meant to paralyze but to galvanize us into action, arming us with the courage to confront our own spiritual battles.

Exorcism, one of the most misunderstood aspects of Catholicism, stands as a testament to the power of faith against the darkest forces. Notable exorcists like Father Gabriele Amorth have shown us the terrifying reality of demonic possession and the monumental victories that come through faith and prayer. These stories aren't mere horror tales; they have been included to place the fear of God in sinners and to inspire steadfastness among the faithful.

Seriousness aside, faith also embraces joy, laughter, and love. Catholicism is rich with humor, and even saints enjoyed a good joke. St. Philip Neri, known for his cheerful spirit, once said, "A joyful heart is more easily made perfect than a downcast one." In our exploration, you will find lighthearted stories that uplift and remind us that joy is a crucial element of spiritual life.

A heart full of repentance is another cornerstone of the journey towards holiness. Stories like the dramatic conversion of St. Paul and the redemption of St. Mary Magdalene serve as timeless reminders of God's infinite mercy. The road to redemption is strewn with obstacles, but these accounts stand as proof that no one is ever beyond the reach of God's grace.

As we delve into the teachings and aphorisms of saints like St. Augustine and St. Teresa of Avila, we will gather pearls of wisdom to guide our everyday lives. These teachings aren't relics of a bygone era but are wonderfully applicable to our contemporary challenges. Paired with proverbs and sayings from the Bible, they serve as a roadmap for living a fulfilling spiritual life.

Furthermore, our faith compels us to love and charity. Acts of kindness by saints such as St. Vincent de Paul and Mother Teresa serve as blueprints for living a life of service.

Their monumental efforts in aiding the poor and marginalized are an ongoing testament to the power of love in action. We also find modern examples of Catholic charity that continue to light the way for willing hearts.

But what happens when life is clouded with despair? The joy of hope, vividly portrayed through stories like that of St. Monica and St. Augustine, is the anchor that holds us steady. In the face of turmoil, these narratives show us how to maintain hope and find solace in God's promise.

Finally, the ultimate goal of this book is to motivate you on the path to righteousness. The importance of evangelization, the transformative power of personal testimonies, and the undying spirit of modern miracles all work together to create a strong spiritual foundation. Encouragement and inspiration will flow through these pages to guide you in bringing others into the fold.

This journey through the labyrinth of faith will not disappoint. The intrepid wanderer will find that it is worth every step, every question, and every moment of doubt. You will emerge from this experience not just as a believer, but as a witness to the incredible power of faith, love, and divine intervention.

So let's embark on this odyssey, shall we? Let's lift the shroud on the mystical, the miraculous, and the mundane, to find wisdom, hope, and a renewed sense of purpose. Together, we will explore the divine encounters, profound teachings, acts of charity, and the overwhelming joy that a fulfilling spiritual life can bring.

May this book serve as a lantern, guiding your steps through both the light and shadow, towards a life of unwavering faith and boundless love.

Chapter 1: The Power of Faith

In the vast tapestry of human experience, faith stands as a singularly transformative force, an elixir for the weary soul and a beacon amid life's darkest storms. Comically insistent, faith refuses to be subdued, popping up like a well-timed jest to provoke smiles in the midst of sorrow. Yet, it also carries a touch of the macabre, threading through tales of saints and sinners like an uninvited specter at a feast. Imagine sturdy souls standing firm, defying despair, and conjuring hope where none seemed possible. This undying faith has wrought miracles that dance between the realms of the marvelously uplifting and the profoundly eerie, challenging the rational mind and quickening the pulse. Through faith, the impossible becomes probable, and so, the faith-filled embark on a peculiar journey where laughter and terror walk hand in hand.

Divine Encounters and Miracles

Throughout history, divine encounters and miracles have served as powerful testimonies to the strength and reality of faith. Though they can sometimes startle or even terrify, these extraordinary events ignite a fervor within the believer's heart, compelling them to see the omnipresent hand of God in the tapestry of human existence. Whether it's a miraculous healing that defies medical explanation or a divine intervention that saved a soul in its darkest hour, these events stand as blaring sirens calling us away from sin and towards the righteousness and wisdom that faith can bestow. Near and far, from ancient saints to modern-day encounters, these miracles are not figments of ancient lore but vivid reminders of a living, breathing God's involvement in our lives. In appreciating these miraculous moments, we gain the strength to persevere, the courage to uplift others, and most importantly, the unwavering resolve to walk the path of righteousness.

Stories of Miracle Healings are a testament to the boundless power of faith and divine intervention. These stories, often surprising and profoundly moving, remind us that when human ingenuity reaches its end, divine mercy begins. They highlight a reality that many find difficult to accept—that the extraordinary sometimes breaks into our ordinary lives, transforming despair into hope, agony into relief, and doubt into faith.

Consider the story of St. John of God, a man who dedicated his life to caring for the sick. When a young boy suffering from a fatal illness was brought to him, the doctors had already given up hope. But St. John refused to accept defeat. He sequestered himself in prayer, beseeching God with a fervor that echoed through the corridors of the makeshift hospital. As the hours passed, the boy's condition inexplicably improved. By morning, he was sitting up, smiling, and asking for food—something deemed impossible the night before. This was not an isolated incident but one of many that solidified St. John's reputation as a healer.

Sometimes, these miracle healings come in the form of a sudden and unexplainable cure. Imagine a mother in the 18th century, clutching the lifeless body of her infant son. She had taken the boy to various physicians, but all had told her the same heart-wrenching news: her son was beyond saving. Desperate, she carried him to the Marian shrine of Our Lady of Good Help in France. Placing him on the altar and praying with a heart full of faith, she left the shrine, convinced of Our Lady's intercession. That evening, the boy awoke, cried, and was filled with life once again. This narrative, while horrifying in its desperation, unfolds into an inspirational testament of divine mercy and a mother's unwavering faith.

Contemporary tales also abound, reinforcing that miracles are not relics of the past but ongoing testament to divine power. Take, for example, the story of a man diagnosed with Stage 4 cancer. Despite undergoing rigorous treatments, he was told his chances were slim. In a final act of faith, he and his wife traveled to Lourdes, hoping for a miracle. They prayed, bathed in the waters, and returned home without any visible sign of healing. Yet, during his next medical examination, doctors found no trace of cancer. This couldn't be explained through conventional medical knowledge, only through the lens of the miraculous. Such stories serve as a reminder that the Age of Miracles is far from over.

There are also miraculous healings that cleanse not just the body, but the soul. St. Damien of Molokai, who served a leper colony in Hawaii, became a symbol of love and courage. Though he eventually succumbed to leprosy himself, his work brought immense spiritual healing to countless individuals. One such man, severely disfigured and ostracized, found new life through St. Damien's touch. Not only did he regain a sense of dignity, but his inward despair was replaced with hope and faith. Damien's intercession didn't just slow the progression of this man's disease; it healed his spirit in ways that resonated far beyond his physical suffering.

In a more modern setting, we have the awe-inspiring account of Chiara, a young woman from Italy, who suffered from chronic and debilitating migraines. Medical treatments failed her, and she endured years of suffering. Driven to the brink of despair, she attended a Mass where relics of St. Rita of Cascia were present. As she prayed, the sharp pain in her head began to fade. By the time the Mass ended, her migraines had completely disappeared. Medical experts were astounded, diagnosing her as miraculously healed. Her faith and the intercession of St. Rita transcended the limitations of medical science.

These stories weave a fabric of inspiration and divine testimony that cannot be ignored. A notable case is that of John Traynor in the early 20th century. A British World War I veteran, John returned home with severe injuries and a life-threatening head wound. Struggling both physically and emotionally, he heard of the miracles of the shrine at

Lourdes. Skeptical but desperate, he made the pilgrimage. Immersing himself in prayer during the procession of the Blessed Sacrament, he felt a sudden warmth envelop his body. Against all odds, he stood up, regained his strength, and walked without assistance. John Traynor returned home, healed, and the medical community could offer no explanation.

Beyond bodily healings, these stories illustrate a profound spiritual dimension. The tale of the paralytic healed by Jesus, as recounted in the Gospel of Mark, resonates with the faithful even today. The Savior's words, "Your sins are forgiven," remind us that true healing transcends physical restoration—it encompasses our entire being. Jesus' miracles were not merely acts of compassion but symbolic gestures pointing to the ultimate healing of humankind through His sacrificial love. This understanding enriches our Catholic faith and encourages a deeper reflection on the relationship between suffering, healing, and redemption.

And who could forget the devotion to St. Padre Pio? Known for his stigmata and the miraculous healings attributed to his intercession, countless testimonials recount ailments—both mundane and terminal—vanishing without a trace. One woman, diagnosed with an incurable blood disease, sought Padre Pio's prayers. As he blessed her, she felt a surge of warmth coursing through her veins. Subsequent medical tests revealed her blood disease had vanished. Such accounts stir the soul, making one question: are these not whispers of God's grace in a skeptical world?

In the tapestry of these miracle stories, humor occasionally finds a way to weave in. Consider the case of a priest in a small village in France, who was well-known not just for his piety but his peculiar sense of humor. When a local man claimed to have been cured of a severe ailment after drinking blessed water, the priest quipped, "It might have been the water, or it might have been the wine you drank with it!" His words, though lighthearted, underscored a profound truth: faith doesn't invalidate reason, but often invites us to look beyond it.

Let's not overlook the transformative experiences of contemporary figures like Mother Teresa, who witnessed miraculous healings in the slums of Calcutta. One such story is of a young man afflicted by severe gangrene. The medical prognosis was amputation, but Mother Teresa, embodying unwavering faith and compassion, prayed over him. Gradually, the gangrene healed, and amputation was no longer necessary. This miraculous recovery wasn't merely a physical healing but a soulful testament to God's mercy, mediated through His humble servant.

Miracle healings, distinct and resplendent as each one is, collectively reflect the timeless interplay of faith and divine intervention. They echo through generations, fortifying the Christian ethos with hope and reverence. They serve as divine reminders that God's mercy, grace, and omnipotence manifest in myriad wondrous ways, inviting both the skeptical and the faithful to witness His infinite love.

Accounts of Divine Intervention are not merely tales of ancient times or distant places. They are the echoes of a celestial symphony playing out in our lives, oftentimes in ways we scarcely realize until we step back and see the divine brushstrokes in the larger canvas of existence. One might even argue that these instances are God's gentle reminders that we're not alone, that the threads of His divine will weave through our lives, binding us closer to His grace.

Consider the story of a fisherman named Pietro from a small coastal village in Italy. Amid one particularly violent storm, his boat capsized, sending him into the frigid waters. Clinging to what little hope he had left, Pietro prayed fervently to St. Anthony. Moments later, a bright light seemed to guide him to a piece of floating debris, enough to keep him afloat until the storm passed and he was miraculously rescued by a passing boat. It wasn't mere chance that saved him that day; faith enshrouded him in divine intervention, pulling him from the jaws of death.

Equally compelling is the tale of Maria, a devout woman from Spain, diagnosed with terminal cancer. Her family, steadfast in their faith, organized a prayer vigil invoking the intercession of St. Jude, the patron saint of lost causes. Over the course of weeks, Maria experienced what could only be described as a miraculous recovery. Her physicians, initially astonished, had no scientific explanation for the unexpected remission. They were left speechless, while Maria's family knew well the source of this divine favor.

Among the more documented cases is that of a young boy named Tomás from the Philippines who fell from a considerable height, landing on a cemented ground. Medical expectations were grim, predicting irreversible brain injuries. However, his parents never wavered in their prayers to Our Lady of Perpetual Help. To the astonishment of the medical staff, Tomás not only woke up but slowly recovered without any long-term damage. Naysayers might attribute it to luck or coincidence, but for those who believe, such events are proof of divine agency at work.

In Irish folklore, there's the fascinating account of Father Francis, who, while traversing the rugged hills, was caught in a violent downpour. His horse lost its footing, and both man and beast tumbled perilously down a steep incline. Unhurt and finding themselves at the bottom unharmed, Father Francis attributed their safety to St. Patrick's protection—a testimony to how divine intervention often manifests in the least likely circumstances and places.

Then there's the extraordinary moment during World War II when a group of soldiers found themselves pinned down by enemy fire in the battlegrounds of Normandy. Facing certain death, they turned their prayers to the Archangel Michael. Seemingly out of nowhere, a dense fog enveloped their position, allowing them to retreat to safety. Such stories aren't merely about survival; they reinforce the belief that the divine watches over humanity, especially when darkness looms close.

The story of Elise, a mother in the United States who had gone missing for days in the wilderness, adds another vivid chapter. Search parties combed through the area without success. Her family, however, sought solace in the power of prayer, appealing to St. Christopher, the patron saint of travelers. On the seventh day, just as hopes began to fade, Elise was discovered unharmed, attributing her survival to a "guardian angel" who led her to a fresh water source and provided her sustenance. Her inexplicable endurance is often whispered as yet another affirmation of divine intervention.

It's not just crises or life-and-death situations where divine interventions occur. Sometimes, they grace our mundane moments, making the ordinary extraordinary. Take for instance the story of a small parish in rural Brazil struggling to gather funds to rebuild their decrepit church. Despite their best efforts, they came up short. One morning, parishioners awoke to find an anonymous donation in the exact amount needed to complete the project. They saw it as heavenly provision, an indication that their prayers had reached divine ears.

Miraculous interventions aren't confined to these dramatic narratives. In various parts of the world, stories abound of people experiencing sudden clarity of purpose, unforeseen forgiveness, or spontaneous peace. There was a man named Raul, who, burdened with an insurmountable grudge, attended a retreat in Fatima. Through communal prayers and meditation, he felt an overwhelming warmth and suddenly, without premeditation, forgave those who wronged him. The turmoil within him dissipated in what he described as an ocean of divine love. Pedantic logic may fail to explain such transformations, but those experiencing them recognize them as moments of divine intervention.

In contemporary times, our heightened reliance on tangible proofs often leads us to overlook these subtle, yet powerful, divine intercessions. The modern world's skepticism cannot dilute the vivid hues of divine artistry within life's grand mural. Divine intervention is like a soft whisper amidst life's chaos, heard only by those attuned to its quiet assurance. These stories serve to remind us of faith's transformative power and the real presence of the divine in our lives.

At its core, divine intervention reinstates the notion that miracles aren't relics of the past but living, breathing manifestations of God's love and mercy. Identifying these instances requires eyes of faith and a heart open to wonders. Whether it's a miraculous escape, a healing touch, or a silent guidance through life's labyrinth, divine intervention continually reassures us that our Creator remains profoundly and lovingly involved in the fabric of our existence.

Chapter 2: Saints and Their Inspiring Lives

Saints, those luminous figures of our faith, offer us a kaleidoscope of inspiration through their profound lives, too rich with grace to be captured in mere words. We look to them, not as unattainable icons, but as compelling examples of holy perseverance in the face of human challenges. Peppered with moments of divine humor, teachings wrapped in layers of motivation, and instances that elicit both awe and reverent fear, their stories serve as poignant reminders of what God can accomplish through those wholly devoted to Him. Whether it's the tangible humility of St. Francis of Assisi, whose very existence seemed a divine jest against materialism, or the Little Flower, St. Therese of Lisieux, whose simple yet profound spirituality dismantles any notion that sanctity is reserved for the grandiose, each narrative lights our own path towards righteousness. Even the lesser-known saints like St. Josephine Bakhita, who turned the horrors of slavery into a triumphant symphony of faith, or St. Andre Bessette, whose quiet devotion healed a multitude, remind us that each soul's journey has the potential for extraordinary holiness. These saints lived not for themselves but for God, thus leaving us a treasure trove of wisdom, a legacy of hope, and a trail illumined for every seeker of truth. And so, armed with their stories, we are fortified to tread boldly on our own paths, aspiring to reign in holiness and charity in a world yearning for such light.

Popular Saints' Stories

In the rich tapestry of Catholic tradition, the lives of saints are threads that shine with divine brilliance. Their stories are not just pious retellings but dynamic epics that ignite our spirits. Take for instance St. Francis of Assisi, who traded a life of wealth for one of humble devotion, bewildering his contemporaries yet inspiring generations of faithful. Then there's St. Therese of Lisieux, whose "little way" of simple, soul-piercing acts of love has brought countless souls closer to divine grace. Each saint's journey, filled with moments of grace and trials alike, beckons us to persevere through our dark nights with courage and humor. As we delve into these tales, we encounter not just historical figures but living beacons of faith who remind us that in our own struggles, we too can find redemption and a path toward the eternal light of God's love.

St. Francis of Assisi has been captivating hearts and minds for centuries, a beacon of humility and a testament to the radical power of faith. He's not just a saint; he's a spiritual dynamo who turned the world on its head. You've probably heard a few of his famous sayings, but behind those pithy phrases is a life filled with extremes—poverty that was more enriching than any treasure, love that knew no bounds, and a zeal that could light the darkest souls.

What makes St. Francis astonishing is how he started—like most saints, he didn't pop out of the womb wearing a halo. Born in 1181, Giovanni di Pietro di Bernardone, known to us as Francis, was the son of a wealthy cloth merchant in Assisi, Italy. He lived the life of a privileged youth, with all the luxuries his father's money could buy. It's almost humorous to think about Saint Francis in silk and finery, perhaps throwing lavish parties. Yet, the Divine has a gloriously ironic sense of humor, and Francis was destined for a radical transformation.

One particular moment stands out: the leper encounter. Picture this—Francis, the son of a rich man, encounters a leper on the road. In those days, lepers were seen as living dead, avoided like the plague—literally. But Francis dismounts from his horse, embraces the man, and kisses him. This wasn't just a moment of charity; it was a divine encounter. As legend has it, the leper was Christ in disguise. This powerful, unsettling moment marked the beginning of Francis's love affair with holy poverty.

Francis's vision for a life of poverty wasn't merely ascetic self-denial; it was a passionate, joyous embodiment of the Beatitudes. Humorously enough, while others were climbing the social ladder, Francis was diving headfirst into humility. He renounced his father's wealth in a public showdown, so memorable it could've been penned by Mark Twain himself. In front of the bishop and an astonished crowd, he stripped off his clothes and declared he had only one Father—our Father in heaven. You could almost hear the gasps and murmurs, a spectacle that was as shocking as it was inspiring.

This act crystallized his commitment to live a life devoid of material possessions. Imagine someone telling you today to give up everything and trust completely in God's providence. Spoiler alert: It's terrifying! But for Francis, it was liberating. He wore a simple tunic, often patched together—donated rags that bore the colors of freedom and divine love.

In another stirring episode, Francis famously preached to the birds. Yes, birds. You might chuckle at the quaintness of such an act, but it was a profound demonstration of his universal love. For Francis, every creature was a reflection of the Creator's glory, a testament to God's endless and boundless love. His sermon to the birds wasn't just a whim; it was pure theology in action. Each chirp and flutter became a hymn of praise.

Francis's life wasn't all pastoral and poetic, though. There were chilling moments too, moments that would chill you to the bone. One evening, in the dead of winter, exhausted and starving, he was found praying at the foot of the snowy Mount Subasio. Francis welcomed suffering as a path to divine intimacy. The stark, icy nights he spent in prayer are reminiscent of the dark nights of the soul Catholics are often reminded of, a time when the only light one has is faith.

Demons tormented him, physical ailments plagued him—he bore the Stigmata, the wounds of Christ, on his body for the last two years of his life. These were signs not merely of suffering but of mystical union with Christ. You can't help but shudder at the idea—yet, for Francis, this was the ultimate expression of love and sacrifice.

Mind you, his fervor wasn't just inward; it was also incredibly outward and infectious. He founded the Franciscan Order along with fellow companions who shared his zeal. The Franciscans were not recluses; they took to the streets, preaching and living among the people. Their very lives were sermons. They didn't just talk about Christ; they lived Christ.

Francis was also deeply devoted to the Eucharist, seeing it as the living Christ in every Mass. He encouraged everyone, from the Pope to the layperson, to revere the Eucharist with profound respect and awe. The Eucharist wasn't just a symbol for him; it was the most direct encounter with Jesus. His reverence was so profound that it reinvigorated the devotion in those around him.

His Canticle of the Sun, a hymn he composed, encapsulates what can only be described as a veritable cosmic dance. In it, he praised God for Brother Sun, Sister Moon, and even Sister Death. It was an all-encompassing adoration that saw no separation between the sacred and the secular. His relationship with God was like a vibrant tapestry that touched every part of existence.

By the time he died in 1226, at the age of 44, Francis had not only lived a transforming life but had initiated a spiritual revolution. His legacy is palpable—he was canonized just two years after his death. But canonization wasn't just a formality; it was a reflection of the indelible mark he left on the Church.

Indeed, St. Francis reignites the faith not through grand theological dissertations but through his life and actions. His life was a sermon, a hymn, a cry of love and devotion. And that's why he resonates so deeply, even today. Francis teaches us that holiness isn't otherworldly; it's profoundly human. It begins with small acts of love, embraces of the untouchable, and a heart that sees Christ in all creation.

So, as we reflect on the life of St. Francis of Assisi, let's remember that our own paths to holiness might be unconventional, maybe even downright shocking, but profoundly beautiful. Let his radical love and deep humility be a mirror to us, guiding our steps as we walk in faith, facing both the light and shadows of our spiritual journeys.

St. Therese of Lisieux is one of those rare saints whose life, though brief, radiates a long-lasting light of love, humility, and simplicity. Born in 1873 in Alençon, France, Therese Martin entered the Carmelite convent in Lisieux at just 15 years old. Her life might seem uneventful at first glance, filled with the mundane routines of monastery life. However, dive deeper, and you'll uncover a treasure trove of spiritual wisdom and profound acts of faith that have inspired countless souls.

Affectionately known as "The Little Flower," St. Therese adopted "the little way" of spiritual childhood, focusing on doing small things with great love instead of grandiose gestures. This approach makes her story especially compelling and accessible. She didn't perform miraculous healings or grand acts of charity, but she transformed routine moments into opportunities for spiritual growth and divine encounter. Imagine living your life where every smile, every chore, every minor inconvenience is turned into an offering to God. That's precisely what

Therese did, and it's a lesson anyone can apply no matter their vocation or station in life.

St. Therese's "Little Way" is fundamentally revolutionary. It's simple yet profound: do ordinary things with extraordinary love. This stands in stark contrast to a world that often prizes ambition, grandeur, and ostentation. As she herself put it, "Our Lord does not so much look at the greatness of our actions, nor even at their difficulty, but at the love with which we do them." This focus on love transforms her seemingly quiet, cloistered existence into a life that echoes across the centuries. The resonance of her teachings can't be overstated.

Despite her young age, or perhaps because of it, she faced her share of trials and tribulations. St. Therese suffered from tuberculosis, a disease that would eventually claim her life at the tender age of 24. Her physical suffering was intense, but it never crushed her spirit. On the contrary, her writings during this period reveal a soul in remarkable harmony with God's will, regardless of the pain she endured. One might say that her short life was a divine paradox—immense suffering paired with immense love.

Her autobiographical work, *The Story of a Soul*, captures her spiritual journey in her own words. This book isn't just an account of her life; it's a spiritual roadmap for anyone wishing to deepen their relationship with God. With touching honesty, she discusses her struggles, doubts, and the small victories that marked her path to holiness. Through her writing, you get the sense that she's inviting every reader into her intimate circle, encouraging them to trust in God's love and mercy.

Let's not forget the miraculous influence of her prayers. Numerous accounts detail how her intercession brought about divine interventions even after her death. Believers have credited her with guiding them through moments of despair, illness, and spiritual crises. In fact, she's often invoked as a saint who sends roses as a sign of answered prayers. Picture this: you're at your wit's end, praying for guidance, and suddenly you encounter an unexpected rose. It's these little miracles that reaffirm faith and inspire deeper devotion to St. Therese's teachings.

But why does her story carry such universal appeal? Perhaps it's because St. Therese's spirituality is exceptionally approachable. She taught that sanctity is accessible to everyone, even those who consider themselves small and insignificant. Her "little way" reassures us that God's love is within reach, no matter where we are on our spiritual journey. Her humility serves as a powerful antidote to the pride that so easily ensnares us. In a world often fixated on success and recognition, Therese speaks to the quiet, authentic pursuit of holiness.

St. Therese of Lisieux was canonized in 1925, and her legacy continues to thrive to this day. Her feast day, celebrated on October 1st, is a time when Catholics worldwide reflect on her life and the simple, yet profound, lessons she imparted. Churches dedicated to her name often house relics, creating a tangible connection to this beloved saint who taught us about the beauty of spiritual childhood and the power of loving God in the little things.

As you meditate on the life of St. Therese, remember that her story isn't just a historical account; it's a call to action. Her "little way" challenges us to reframe our lives, not in terms of grand achievements, but in the sincerity and love we bring to our everyday tasks. From cleaning your home to managing your work, every moment becomes an opportunity to live out the Gospel in tiny, transformative ways.

So, go ahead, embrace the "little way" in your own life. Transform your daily routines into acts of love, just as St. Therese did. In doing so, you'll discover the profound joy and peace that comes from living in harmony with God's will. After all, in the eyes of God, there are no small acts of love; each one is a step closer to eternity.

Lesser-Known Saints

While the tales of well-known saints like St. Francis of Assisi and St. Therese of Lisieux often steal the spotlight, the lives of lesser-known saints such as St. Josephine Bakhita and St. Andre Bessette offer profound lessons and inspirations. St. Josephine Bakhita, once a slave, embraced her suffering with a spirit of forgiveness and unwavering faith, turning her chains into a testament of God's redemptive love. Similarly, St. Andre Bessette, a humble doorkeeper with a robust devotion to St. Joseph, performed miraculous healings that defied worldly explanations. These saints walked paths paved with adversity, yet transformed their trials into triumphs of divine faith. Their stories serve as poignant reminders that sainthood doesn't demand grandeur but rather a heart wholly surrendered to God's will, embodying the silent, powerful call to holiness each of us carries.

St. Josephine Bakhita holds a luminous place in the tapestry of our faith, her life a poignant testament to the redemptive power of God's grace. Born around 1869 in the region of Darfur in Sudan, Bakhita's early life was marked by unimaginable tribulations. At the tender age of seven, she was kidnapped by Arab slave traders, an ordeal that would see her sold and resold over twelve times, subjected to brutal treatment that could break anyone's spirit.

Yet, instead of succumbing to despair, St. Josephine Bakhita found a connection with the divine. In one of the most harrowing periods of her life, she was 'tattooed' with a knife—an excruciating process where a pattern was carved into her skin and salt rubbed into the wounds. It's nothing short of miraculous that during such suffering, she developed a profound sense of God's presence, an inner strength that physical pain could not annihilate. There's a spine-chilling reminder here of the profound resilience of the human soul when touched by divine grace.

In her teens, Bakhita was finally sold to an Italian diplomat, Callisto Legnani, and for the first time began experiencing kindness and compassion. When Legnani returned to Italy, he took Bakhita with him, and it was here that her life took a transformative turn. She was entrusted to the Canossian Sisters in Venice during a period when her master was away. Exposure to the Catholic faith ignited something deep within her. Despite facing significant cultural and emotional hurdles, Bakhita felt drawn inexplicably toward the teachings of Christ.

In 1890, she was baptized and confirmed, taking the name Josephine Margaret Bakhita. The Sisters taught her about the love of God, a love that saw her not as a commodity but as a person of incalculable worth. Imagine, for a moment, the enormity of this paradigm shift for Bakhita—it was like emerging from darkness into the brightest of lights. Baptism not only cleansed her of original sin but marked the beginning of her new life in Christ. Her joy and inner peace became palpable, resonating with those who encountered her.

When Legnani returned to reclaim her, the now Catholic Bakhita faced another battle, not with physical chains but against the shackles of ownership that denied her human dignity. With the help of the Canossian Sisters and a ruling from the Italian courts, she won her freedom. Bakhita's victory became a manifestation of divine justice on Earth, an example of the Lord's intervention in breaking the literal and metaphorical chains that bind us.

Free at last, St. Josephine chose to dedicate her life to the very order that helped her find salvation. She joined the Canossian Daughters of Charity in 1896. For the next fifty years, she served in various capacities, from cooking to being a portress, but regardless of her roles, her life became a living prayer, a symphony of love and service seasoned with humor and compassion. It wasn't just her work that inspired; it was her unwavering faith and joy, even amidst prior suffering. Her spirit seemed unbreakable, a beacon for anyone grappling with their own burdens.

Bakhita would often say, "Be good, love the Lord, pray for those who do not know Him. What a great grace it is to know God!" Simple words, yet pregnant with profound wisdom and the sweet, spicy flavor of a lived experience that all can taste and see. Her advices weren't wrapped in heavy theology but in the simplicity of deep, heartfelt truth. Her faith and charitable acts were the antithesis of the horror she endured, embodying the Church's mission to be Christ's hands and feet in this world.

St. Josephine Bakhita's life also compels us to examine our own chains—whether they be sin, addiction, or spiritual complacency. Are we willing to confront them with the same tenacity she displayed, trusting in God's unyielding love to guide us through the darkest valleys? In Bakhita's narrative, we find a motivational anthem to persevere, not through sheer willpower alone, but through anchoring oneself firmly in faith.

Her story has a haunting yet invigorating resonance today, especially in an era rampant with modern forms of slavery and human trafficking. While technological advancements have catapulted society forward, certain vile practices stubbornly persist, cloaked in new guises. Bakhita's canonization in 2000 by Pope John Paul II was not merely a veneration of her personal sanctity but a clarion call to combat injustice in all its loathsome forms.

In the twilight of her life, she endured a prolonged illness, bearing her suffering with remarkable grace until she was called home on February 8, 1947. Her relics now rest in Schio, Italy, where countless devotees come to seek her intercession. In these encounters, her legacy lives on, a perpetual incense offering before God, mingling with the prayers of the faithful worldwide.

As Roman Catholics, reflecting on St. Josephine Bakhita's life, we are invited to a deeper commitment to acts of charity and empathy. Knowing her story, how can we remain indifferent to the plight of others? How can her radiant example not inspire us to extend the same compassion and love that transformed her life to those around us? Bakhita may not have penned elaborate theological treatises, but her life itself is a compelling homily, urging us to be the salt of the earth and the light of the world.

Let her example be a brilliant reminder that no matter how monstrous our trials may appear, God's mercy is always greater. Through the life of **St. Josephine Bakhita,** we witness a glorious tapestry woven from the threads of pain, resilience, redemption, and ultimately, enduring joy in the Lord. So, let us march forward, emboldened by her example, ever ready to fight the good fight with the same fervent faith and unwavering hope that characterized her extraordinary journey.

St. Andre Bessette was a beacon of hope to the faithful, a quiet giant who turned the mundane into miraculous. Nothing about his early life suggested he would become a saint. Born Alfred Bessette in 1845, this future hero of faith started his journey in humble beginnings in Quebec, Canada. Orphaned at the age of twelve, he faced adversity head-on, working various jobs to survive. Alfred was a frail boy, often beset by illness, but his spiritual vigor was boundless.

One can imagine the laughter and skepticism that greeted his entrance into the Congregation of Holy Cross in 1870. He was tasked with the most pedestrian of responsibilities— a porter, or doorman, at Notre Dame College in Montreal. Ah, but God loves to use the lowly to confound the mighty! Andre, as he was now known, took his duties seriously, greeting visitors with a humility and kindness that belied his hidden strength. Through the simplicity of his role, he demonstrated that sanctity does not require grandeur, just a heart full of faith.

Andre's true vocation bloomed as people began noticing his deep devotion to St. Joseph. The sick and suffering flocked to him, and stories of miraculous healings began to spread. Yet, he always deflected praise, insisting that it was St. Joseph who performed these wonders. As the tales multiplied, one couldn't help but ponder: was it irony or divine design that the weakest of men wielded such powerful intercession?

Even in his own lifetime, St. Andre's deeds seemed to dance between the realms of humor and horror. Imagine the scene: throngs of ailing pilgrims clutching his cloak, hoping for a touch of divine mercy, while the solemn stares of skeptics hovered in the shadows. Yet, with unyielding compassion, Andre moved through the multitudes, never breaking stride in his humble tasks. One struck by his faith might feel stirred to laughter at the audacity of such belief, or frozen in awe at the palpable presence of divine intervention.

Andre's influence grew beyond Notre Dame College's gates. By 1904, he had a small oratory built, dedicated to St. Joseph. It was the beginnings of what would become the renowned Saint Joseph's Oratory of Mount Royal, Canada's largest church dedicated to the foster father of Jesus. But André's vision wasn't just to create a monumental structure—he longed to foster an equally monumental faith within the hearts of the people.

As miracle after miracle was reported, the Oratory became a beacon for the desperate. Crutches, once supporting anguished bodies, now covered the walls as silent testimonies to the power of intercession. Consider, for a moment: what would it be like to walk among those walls, feeling the invisible strength that turned prayers into palpable realities? It's equal parts eerie and exhilarating.

In 1937, after a long life of service, Andre passed away at the age of 91. His funeral drew over a million mourners, a clear testament to the lives he had touched. The humor in this celestial irony was not lost— here was an orphaned, sickly boy who transformed into a spiritual titan. It's enough to make one chuckle at how unpredictable God's plans can be, even while being awed by their intricate wisdom.

This legacy, however, did not end with his death. In 1960, years after his passing, the Oratory's basilica construction was completed, standing as a magnificent beacon of faith inspired by a man who worked in its corridors as a humble doorman. This monumental site, heavy with history and laden with miracles, continues to draw millions seeking hope and healing.

St. Andre Bessette's life offers a masterclass in quiet resilience and faith. His humility, commitment, and sense of humor in the face of adversity inspire us today. Picture him, an ailing boy turned porter-turned-saint, smiling softly as he directs all acclaim heavenward. He wasn't a warrior in the traditional sense, yet he fought spiritual battles with the armor of faith and the shield of humility.

Such stories of strength and grace encourage us to follow his footsteps. Like Andre, we might feel like mere porters in life's grand hotel, overwhelmed and undervalued. Yet, his life teaches us that even the most modest of us can channel divine power and perform wonders by embracing humility and unwavering trust in God. This calls us to reflect: How can we, in our everyday lives, act as conduits for divine grace and mercy? St. Andre's example is clear—through love, faith, and the honest execution of our humble duties, we too can create a lasting impact.

As we traverse our spiritual journeys, let St. Andre Bessette guide us as a beacon of hope, faith, and boundless possibility. His life reminds us that sanctity lies not in grand acts but in the faithful execution of small, loving deeds done with great faith. Therein lies the path to righteousness and wisdom, where even the simplest doorman can open the gates to heaven.

Chapter 3: Visionaries and Mystics

The annals of faith are replete with the harrowing and awe-inspiring experiences of visionaries and mystics. These individuals stand at the intersection of the divine and the earthly, often bearing messages too profound and unsettling for the mundane world. From the tender revelations of the Blessed Virgin Mary, who graced humble souls with her celestial presence, to the prophetic dreams of St. John Bosco, these encounters serve as both a balm and a jolt to our spiritual consciousness. They compel us to confront the eternal truths of our faith with renewed vigor, blending the sweet comfort of divine love with the chilling reminder of our earthly trials. Prepare to be both exhorted and enlightened, as these potent narratives of visionary experiences probe deeply into the realms of heaven, purgatory, and, yes, even the terrifying abysses of hell. With humor's light touch and the gravity of eternal consequences, it's an invitation to walk the perilous yet profoundly rewarding path of the faithful.

Saints' Visions

In a world teetering between grace and calamity, saints' visions stand as a testament to the divine reaching out to humanity, compelling us to glimpse beyond the veil of our daily existence. These holy individuals, often misunderstood and dismissed in their own time, were bearers of sacred messages that reveal both the sublime beauty and the harrowing truths of the spiritual realm. Take, for instance, St. John Bosco's prophetic dreams that navigated the treacherous seas of sin and redemption with equal parts dread and hope, each night a cosmic drama unfolding within the theater of his soul. Or consider the piercingly vivid apparitions of the Blessed Virgin Mary, who appeared not for trivial comfort but to provoke the conscience, calling sinners to repentance and believers to a deeper faith. These visions aren't mere relics of a bygone era; they are echoes of a divine wisdom that challenge us to live righteously and embrace the awe-inspiring mysteries of our Faith with a heart alight with holy fear and inspirational fervor.

Apparitions of the Blessed Virgin Mary have a unique and captivating place in the hearts of the faithful. These Divine encounters inspire reverence, hope, and sometimes a bit of terror. From Fatima to Lourdes, the Blessed Virgin has appeared to shepherds, visionaries, and ordinary people, bringing heavenly messages that transcend the ordinary.

Take the apparitions at Fatima, for instance. In the thick of World War I, when Portugal was not spared from the chaos, three shepherd children—Lucia, Jacinta, and Francisco—experienced something extraordinary in 1917. They reported seeing a "Lady more brilliant than the sun," a vision that not only warmed their hearts but also cast shadows of mystery and urgency. With subsequent apparitions delivering prophetic messages about war, peace, and perhaps most chillingly, the vision of Hell, it's clear that these experiences aimed to jar people from spiritual complacency, igniting a fervor for repentance and prayer.

Then there's Lourdes, where another humble girl, Bernadette Soubirous, witnessed multiple apparitions of the Blessed Virgin in 1858. Unlike Fatima, which felt laced with apocalyptic warnings, Lourdes delivered a serene message of healing. Bernadette was instructed to drink from a spring that miraculously appeared, a spring that continues to draw millions of pilgrims to this day, seeking physical and spiritual cures. Who could resist the allure of a place where Heaven itself seemed to have kissed earth?

Our Lady of Guadalupe's apparition to Juan Diego in 1531 unfolds like a tale infused with cultural and spiritual renewal. Juan Diego, a simple indigenous man, encountered a woman shining in radiant beauty atop Tepayac Hill. She identified herself as the Mother of God and asked for a church to be built in her honor. The story takes an awe-inspiring turn with the miraculous image imprinted on Juan Diego's tilma, which in itself is a fascinating weave of divine artistry and symbolism.

Each apparition presents a tableau of faith and mysticism that grips your soul. Who wouldn't feel a shiver of awe upon hearing how children, oftentimes the most unassuming and pure among us, become the chosen mouthpieces for these celestial messages? Yet, with these appearances comes a sobering message—warnings aimed at a deeply divided and spiritually slumbering world. These aren't just simple sightings but profound calls to action.

The why and how of these apparitions often remain shrouded in divine mystery. Why three shepherd children in a Portuguese field? Why an indigenous convert on a Mexican hill? It's as if Heaven itself chooses its canvases with purpose, picking the humble, the meek, those whom the world might deem insignificant, to become pivotal characters in a celestial narrative aimed at humanity's heart.

Consider apparitions like those at Medjugorje, ongoing since the early 1980s, where six visionaries have recounted messages emphasizing prayer, conversion, and peace. Hundreds of millions have visited this small

Bosnia and Herzegovina village, trekking through rocky paths and spiritual turmoil, seeking a glimpse of divine grace in their troubled lives. These apparitions, much like the others, sprinkle a mix of divine mystery and human yearning into the everyday fabric of our lives.

It's not always easy to embrace these messages. There's a natural skepticism, even among the faithful. Yet, it's precisely this tension that adds layers of authenticity and urgency. After all, true faith often rests in the uncomfortable balance between doubt and belief. Those who witness apparitions are rarely left unchanged, and their stories carry a deep resonance that impacts believers around the globe.

For the Catholic in search of faith and truth, these apparitions serve as touchstones. They offer a blend of holy warnings and celestial comfort, pushing us toward a life of diligent faith and earnest conversion. When we read about these miraculous events, we aren't just consuming stories but are invited to become part of a larger narrative—a spiritual drama that challenges and sustains us in equal measure.

Warnings of war, visions of Hell, assurances of divine mercy—these elements are like compass points, guiding humanity through the foggy terrains of moral and spiritual life. The apparitions of the Blessed Virgin Mary compel us to reflect, to repent, and to strive for a greater devotion that transcends the mundane. In these moments of divine encounter, we're nudged, sometimes forcefully, toward a fuller, more potent experience of our faith.

These apparitions often emphasize the importance of the Rosary, penance, and the conversion of sinners. Through seemingly simple requests, profound changes are set into motion. Consider the Rosary; it transforms from a string of beads into a lifeline, connecting Heaven and Earth, binding the faithful in a unified plea for divine intercession. Penance isn't just an act of self-mortification but a pathway to spiritual renewal, a way to align ourselves closer to God's will.

Understandably, the fear of God is a recurring theme in these apparitions. But it's not a fear rooted in terror; rather, it's a reverent awe, an acknowledgment of the omnipotent force that governs us all. When the Blessed Virgin Mary appears with urgent messages, we are reminded of our mortality, our failings, and the tremendous capacity for grace and redemption available to us.

The emotional landscape of these apparitions is vast—hope, fear, joy, penance. Visionaries often describe an overwhelming sense of peace, even when their messages are sobering. This dichotomy captures the essence of the spiritual life itself: a journey fraught with trials but underpinned by an unshakeable, divine hope.

Whether you find solace in Lourdes or urgency in Fatima, the core message remains consistent: Convert, repent, and hold steadfast in your faith. Each apparition serves as a celestial nudge, pushing the faithful toward spiritual growth and deeper communion. The Blessed Virgin Mary, in her manifold appearances, becomes both a tender mother and an urgent prophet, guiding us through the labyrinth of our spiritual journeys.

Despite the differences in their messages, each apparition reinforces the ultimate call to holiness and conversion. They serve as both a mirror and a lamp—reflecting our flaws while lighting the path to redemption and grace. The faithful are encouraged to heed these Divine calls with the seriousness they deserve, while also finding inspiration in their compassionate guidance.

The apparitions of the Blessed Virgin Mary stand as a testament to the enduring bond between Heaven and humanity, offering glimpses of the divine amidst earthly turmoil. They are profound reminders of the eternal truths enshrined in the heart of our faith, urging us towards a deeper, more fervent commitment to the path of righteousness and divine wisdom.

St. John Bosco's Prophetic Dreams were no ordinary flights of fancy; they were windows into the divine, filled with startling clarity and forewarning. The man himself, Don Bosco, foresaw the future with such lucidity that it shook many who heard his accounts. His dreams often surpassed the bounds of human conception, intertwining the fate of individuals and society with a transcendental narrative that only faith could untangle.

The first dream of prophetic significance that St. John Bosco experienced was when he was just a boy. Imagine a young lad, no more than nine, dreaming of a vast field filled with a multitude of wild animals. Suddenly, an ethereal figure appears, transforming the snarling beasts into gentle lambs. The figure, who identifies Himself as Jesus, instructs John to lead these lambs. This early vision set the stage for Bosco's future mission - the conversion and education of wayward youth.

For those drifting away from the Church, Bosco's dreams served as both a lantern and a warning bell. One notable dream occurred in

1861, a peculiar vision revealing two great pillars in the sea, capped by the Holy Eucharist and the Blessed Virgin Mary. Between these pillars swung a colossal ship, beset by hostile vessels. The ship represented the Church; the pillars, its anchors. Through this allegory, Bosco perceived the political and spiritual storms that would challenge the Church. His message was clear: the Church must remain anchored to these divine pillars to survive the tumult.

But not all of Bosco's visions were shrouded in symbolism. Some were stark and terrifyingly direct. In one particularly chilling dream, he found himself witnessing a vast, decrepit castle, filled with wayward youths. As he ventured further, Bosco encountered a horrid figure, the embodiment of evil, draped in cold malice. From its mouth spilled a horde of serpents, whispering deceit into the ears of the unsuspecting. This was a vision of hell, pure and vivid, and it compelled Bosco to double his efforts in guiding these souls back to the path of righteousness.

The dreams were also poignant maps of warning for his dear students. In one heart-wrenching dream, Bosco foresaw the untimely death of a young boy, Charles, if he did not renounce his wayward ways. Deeply moved, Bosco confronted the boy, and after much exhortation, Charles amended his life. The dream's prophecy was averted, and Charles went on to live a longer, holier life. Such instances were not mere coincidence but divine interventions meticulously woven through Bosco's dreams.

St. John Bosco did not interpret these dreams in isolation. He shared them with his close confidants and spiritual directors, who often confirmed their divine origins. These dreams were not meant to be cloistered within the recesses of his mind but shared to awaken the faithful and shield them from spiritual perils. His fellow priests and followers found in these recountings a profound source of spiritual reinforcement and guidance.

The enigmatic nature of Bosco's dreams extends beyond mere narrative. They inhabit a spiritual dimension where the corporeal and the divine entwine, serving as a conduit between earth and heaven. In many dreams, Bosco stood at crossroads, faced with choices that held collective fates in balance. Visualize him on a narrow path, edged with thorns and serpents, and know these are not mere figments but realities of our moral journey.

Bosco's most haunting dreams were those concerning his own community's spiritual well-being. He dreamt of labyrinthine paths filled with pitfalls, representing the temptations and trials his pupils would face. In one striking dream, he recalled a field blanketed with rose petals. As his boys rushed to reach the petals, hidden thorns beneath the roses ensnared them. The roses symbolized worldly pleasures, enticing but perilous. No soul was beyond reach for Don Bosco, and each dream fortified his resolve to guide every boy safely through those lurking spiritual thorns.

In an even more dramatic account, Bosco dreamt of a vast plain where a sinister figure led a herd of ignorant sheep toward a cliff. As the sheep reached the edge, they plummeted into an abyss. The imagery was stark: Satan leading souls to perdition. Bosco's mission was rendered urgent. These visions were fuel for his tireless work; they were divine nudges keeping the urgency of his purpose at the forefront of his mind.

Without a doubt, Bosco's most entire life was a living testament to the efficacy and seriousness of his dreams. Take, for instance, his Dream of the Two Columns, which served as a potent illustration of his ecclesiastical teachings. In one vision, he saw the Church represented as a ship in turmoil, navigated safely by the twin columns of the Eucharist and the Virgin Mary. This vivid representation stressed the spiritual anchor points that kept him, and the faithful, afloat amidst the stormiest seas.

The lessons drawn from St. John Bosco's prophetic dreams are as relevant today as they were in his time. They beckon us to remain steadfast in our faith, ever-vigilant of the moral pitfalls before us. They remind us of the profound spiritual battles being waged beyond our sight and the strength we draw from divine connections - the Holy Eucharist and the intercession of the Blessed Virgin Mary. Each dream is a chapter in a much larger spiritual narrative, one that invites readers to immerse themselves fully in the lived experience of faith.

Intriguingly, Bosco did not see these visions solely as personal revelations but communal edifications. He shared them to build a collective spiritual consciousness. His recounting of these dreams often left listeners in awe, urging them to introspect and strengthen their spiritual armory. The wisdom and foresight encapsulated in these dreams transcended Bosco's era, offering enduring lessons and warnings that reverberate through the halls of Catholic doctrine.

St. John Bosco's prophetic dreams, therefore, were not confined to the realms of mysticism but stretched into the practical domains of life and morality. They acted as guiding stars, urging the faithful towards paths of virtue, penance, and spiritual anchorage.

Through them, the divine reached out to humanity, reminding them of the celestial stakes at play in life's every decision. These dreams remain an evergreen testament to the profound synergy between the celestial and the terrestrial, urging steadfastness, repentance, and divine fidelity.

mystical experiences from purgatory and hell

In the haunting shadows of purgatory and the fiery depths of hell, many visionaries and mystics have witnessed sights that both chill the bone and inspire the soul. St. Catherine of Genoa's intense visions painted purgatory as a realm where divine mercy and justice intersect, sparking a sense of hope amidst suffering. Blessed Anne Catherine Emmerich's vivid accounts of hell, on the other hand, revealed the terrifying consequences of sin, igniting a fervent urgency for repentance and conversion. These mystical experiences, though laden with horror, serve a grander purpose: they remind us of the power of divine justice, the importance of penance, and the ultimate journey toward salvation. By embracing these revelations with both caution and hope, the faithful can find the strength to persevere in their spiritual battles, guided by the wisdom of those who have glimpsed the afterlife's profound mysteries.

St. Catherine of Genoa's Visions Visions are often the keyhole through which we peer into the divine mysteries, and St. Catherine of Genoa's extraordinary experiences provide just that. Not merely fleeting dreams or vague impressions, her visions were stark, intense, and at times, overwhelmingly terrifying. They gnawed at the edges of human understanding and painted a picture far removed from the mundane reality we inhabit. To explore her visions is to dive into a different realm, one where the fabric of spiritual truth is both vibrant and chilling.

Born in 1447, St. Catherine of Genoa's life was a turbulent mix of personal struggles and profound spiritual insights. Her visions provided her not just with a sense of divine closeness but also a harrowing glimpse into the realities of the afterlife—most notably, Purgatory and Hell. These weren't casual visions you could brush off; they were vivid, haunting testimonies that served as both a cautionary tale and a beacon of light for the faithful.

Imagine, if you will, walking into a room filled with blinding light and oppressive darkness simultaneously. That's the spiritual tension St. Catherine navigated. Her visions of Purgatory revealed souls in states of various suffering, yet paradoxically, bathed in divine love. It's hard to picture, isn't it? The souls she saw were not abandoned; they underwent purifying flames that, while painful, were leading them towards eternal joy. For St. Catherine, Purgatory was not just a place of torment but a realm of transformative love where souls were willingly purified.

One might think that experiencing these visions would harden a heart, yet for St. Catherine, they had the opposite effect. These spiritual encounters deepened her empathy and fueled her desire to pray for those suffering souls. She saw Purgatory not merely as a place of punishment, but as an extension of God's boundless mercy. Her revelations compel us to consider how suffering might serve a purgative purpose, not just in the afterlife, but in our earthly lives as well.

Transitioning from Purgatory to Hell, St. Catherine's visions grew darker, more visceral. While Purgatory was painful but hopeful, Hell was utter desolation. Imagine a reality devoid of hope, where divine love is a distant memory, replaced by an eternity of despair. Her visions of Hell were filled with anguished souls, tormented not just by external flames but by the inner fire of regret and separation from God. These souls, bound by their choices, suffered endlessly, a stark reminder to cherish and safeguard one's soul.

Despite the ghastly nature of these visions, St. Catherine retained a sense of divine justice and compassion. She didn't see the damned as mere victims of God's wrath; instead, they were souls who, through persistent rejection of God's grace, had chosen this eternal separation. There's a chilling accountability here—a testament to the ultimate importance of our earthly decisions.

St. Catherine's visions weren't just meant to terrify but to awaken. Are you trembling yet? Good. It's a reminder of what's at stake. The purpose of these divine encounters was to stir the hearts of the indifferent, lighting a fire under those who may have grown complacent. Sin carries weight, and St. Catherine's insights serve as a stark call to repentance.

Yet, there's hope woven into her visions. In depicting such harrowing images, St. Catherine also presents the availability of divine mercy. Remember, her revelations weren't to condemn but to call sinners back to the path of righteousness. Her life, fraught with her own struggles and eventual spiritual triumph, serves as a living testament to God's endless grace.

And what about you? Will you heed her visions and take action? Will you do more than just fear the inferno, and instead, turn that fear into meaningful change? St. Catherine would undoubtedly urge us to seek confession, to cleanse our souls, and to live each day as if it were a step closer to meeting the divine.

From a lighter perspective, it's almost humorous how human we are, continually needing celestial wake-up calls to keep us on track. Whether it's because we're stubborn or simply too absorbed in our daily lives, we occasionally need saints like Catherine to shake us out of our spiritual lethargy. These visions aren't relics of the past; they are lessons for the present, urging us toward repentance and a deeper relationship with God.

Even as we ponder the terrifying realities she describes, there's also an incredible sense of motivation embedded within St. Catherine's visions. They push us to strive for holiness, to seek God's grace more fervently. We aren't merely being scared straight; we're being led into the arms of divine love, purified, much like those souls in Purgatory.

In wrapping our minds around these intense revelations, it's crucial to remember that St. Catherine saw everything through the lens of God's infinite mercy. Despite the horrors of Purgatory and Hell, her visions reinforced

God's ongoing invitation to redemption. No matter where we stand now, we are never beyond the reach of heavenly grace. Her message hits home: transform fear into fervor, guilt into goodness, and lose no time in seeking God's love.

As we delve deeper into the lives of other saints and their mystical experiences, St. Catherine of Genoa's visions remain a pivotal reminder. They stir within us a renewed desire for repentance and a reverent fear of divine justice. Her story is not one to merely read and forget, but one to meditate upon, letting its spiritual gravity shape our actions and souls.

Blessed Anne Catherine Emmerich's Accounts

capture the imagination in a way that few other mystical narratives can. Her experiences, vivid and mystifying, offer both comfort and eerie admonitions to those on the journey of faith. Often bed-ridden and frail in her earthly existence, Emmerich was extraordinarily active in her spiritual life, roaming landscapes both heavenly and infernal through her visionary experiences. These aren't mere flights of fancy but meticulously detailed and hauntingly specific occurrences that provide unique spiritual insights and warnings.

Born in 1774 in Germany, Blessed Anne Catherine Emmerich spent her youth in humble surroundings. She entered the convent at twenty-eight, taking her vows and committing herself to a life of prayer and penance. Her frail health seemed almost to contradict the power of her spiritual visions—appearances of Jesus, Mary, and even realms beyond human comprehension. The manner in which she would recount these visions, often from a state of ecstatic trance, left those who heard her spellbound. They seemed like windows into a metaphysical realm that believers often struggle to imagine, let alone understand.

One of the most captivating aspects of Emmerich's visions was her detailed descriptions of purgatory and hell. These aren't pleasant tea-time stories but rather stern reminders of the realities of sin and divine justice. Emmerich saw souls suffering in purgatory, urged on by their penitence yet tormented by the sins they had committed in life. What makes her accounts particularly gripping is her compassionate perspective. She felt the pain of these souls, sharing it with an almost maternal concern, pleading with the living to remember the dead in their prayers and masses. It wasn't just about fear; it was a manifestation of deep spiritual solidarity between the living and the departed.

Equally unsettling were her glimpses into hell itself. Emmerich described this hellish domain in a manner that would make even the most stoic feel a chill up their spine. She saw the damned—souls who had obstinately rejected divine mercy—existing in utter torment, separated from God for eternity. For her, these weren't sadistic tales to frighten children but a real spiritual urgency to echo Christ's call for repentance. It paints a stark contrast between divine justice and mercy, the latter always extending its hand but the former emphatically real for those who spurn it.

Interestingly, her visions weren't always dark and foreboding. She had remarkable experiences of encounters with heavenly beings and saints. Visiting the realms of the blessed, she saw luminous landscapes where peace, joy, and love reigned supreme. She met saints and angels who encouraged her, imparting divine wisdom and offering glimpses of the eternal beauty awaiting the faithful. These heavenly visions were a stark contrast to the grim scenes from purgatory and hell, reminding us of the rewards promised in Scripture for those who persevere in righteousness.

Emmerich's life was layered with mystical occurrences that defy simple explanation.

Apart from her visions, she reportedly bore the stigmata—the wounds of Christ—on her body. This divine mark served as a visual testament to her extraordinary communion with Christ's suffering. Skeptics might argue against such phenomena, but for those who follow her journey, it becomes a compelling argument for the depth and mystery of divine experiences.

What stands out remarkably in Emmerich's accounts is her unshakable faith amidst adversity. The visions didn't merely provide information; they were transformative experiences that deepened her humility and trust in God. Blessed Anne Catherine Emmerich serves as a bridge between the physical and spiritual worlds. Through her narratives, she holds a mirror up to each soul, reflecting the eternal consequences of earthly actions while also offering a path to divine mercy and grace.

Her visions of the Passion of Christ are particularly poignant and heart-rending. These images are awash in blood and agony, depicting Christ's suffering in excruciating detail. Yet, they also convey the infinite love and sacrifice that underpin the Christian faith. Emmerich felt not just sorrow but a profound sense of participation in Christ's redemptive act. Anyone reading her accounts can't help but be moved, horrified at the extent of human cruelty but equally astonished by the depth of divine love.

The Church has recognized the spiritual value of Emmerich's visions while also cautioning against taking them as literal gospel. Although her accounts must pass through the filter of doctrinal scrutiny, they serve as exceptional sources of reflection and meditation. They invite believers to pray more fervently, live more righteously, and view their struggles in light of an eternal destiny orchestrated by divine will.

In our age, where skepticism and secularism often overshadow spiritual truths, Blessed Anne Catherine Emmerich's accounts regain their urgent relevance. Her life and visions serve as a humbling reminder of the unseen realities that intersect our mundane existence. In Evangelii Gaudium, Pope Francis emphasizes the need to rejuvenate the spirit of evangelization. Emmerich's accounts, brimming with both horror and hope, act as powerful catalysts for this spiritual renewal. Whether contemplating the ghastly torments of the damned or the sublime glory of the blessed, one is compelled towards a deeper, more fervent spiritual life.

In essence, Blessed Anne Catherine Emmerich's accounts bring forth the most critical aspects of Christian faith—justice, mercy, repentance, and divine love—in a manner that is both terrifying and awe-inspiring. They challenge us to reflect on the reality of sin, the urgency of repentance, and the boundless treasures of divine grace. Her visions are a choir of divine whispers mingled with solemn warnings, urging us to strive for heaven while we still have time on this earth.

Chapter 4: The Role of Exorcists in Spiritual Warfare

Exorcists are the Church's front-line soldiers in the unseen battle against spiritual darkness, wielding sacramental authority like a double-edged sword forged in prayer and divine mandate. Their role, often shrouded in mystery and fear, is one of steadfast bravery and unwavering faith, confronting malevolent forces that seek to corrupt and enslave souls. Far from the stuff of mere legend or Hollywood fantasy, these spiritual warriors engage in a grim yet profoundly necessary mission—dispelling the dominion of evil with the light of Christ. While their rites may appear archaic to the modern skeptic, to the faithful, they are a powerful affirmation of the Church's enduring might against the infernal. Through the rigors of solemn exorcisms and quiet deliverances alike, exorcists remind us all that no soul is beyond redemption, and no darkness can withstand the power of God.

Understanding Exorcism

Understanding exorcism requires us to venture into the stark realities of spiritual warfare, where the clash between good and evil isn't just allegorical, but startlingly literal. Exorcism is the Church's potent response to the unsettling manifestations of diabolical influence, a sacred confrontation that embodies courage, faith, and divine authority. It's a solemn ritual, steeped in ancient tradition and fortified by prayer, designed to liberate souls from the grips of malevolent forces. While some might view exorcism through the prism of horror and disbelief, for the faithful, it is a testament to God's enduring power and mercy. Those undergoing these harrowing experiences emerge not just as survivors, but as living proofs of the triumph of divine light over darkness, urging us all to strengthen our spiritual defenses and trust deeply in the mighty deliverance that comes from faith.

The Rite of Exorcism Explained is one of the most misunderstood practices in the Catholic Church. Some think of it as an ancient, dramatized ritual meant for horror movies; others believe it's an obsolete rite from a bygone era. However, it remains a solemn and pivotal element in the Church's mission of spiritual warfare.

The Rite of Exorcism isn't a recent invention but has its roots deep in Christian history. For those wrestling with the malevolent presence of evil, it offers a beacon of hope and divine intervention. The rite aims to liberate individuals from demonic possession, a term loaded with connotations that evoke both fear and fascination.

At its core, exorcism is about asserting the authority of Jesus Christ over evil. When a person is believed to be possessed, an exorcist—usually a priest appointed by the bishop—invokes the name of Jesus, various saints, and the power of sacred scripture. This rite acts like a divine lifeline, pulling the afflicted back from the brink of spiritual destruction.

The process begins with an exhaustive investigation. A priest must discern between mental illness and genuine demonic possession. This step is critical and not taken lightly. Modern psychology and medicine play a role here; the Church collaborates with medical professionals to rule out any natural explanations before proceeding with the rite. When science finds no plausible answers, the case is escalated to an exorcist.

Once possession is confirmed, the real battle begins. This is no Hollywood spectacle but a harrowing, spiritual encounter. The priest-administrator of the ritual prepares by attending Mass, fasting, and praying fervently. The exorcist often recites specific prayers, called "the exorcisms," part of a sacred text known as the Roman Ritual. These prayers explicitly reject the devil, invoke saints, and command the demon to leave the possessed individual.

What does this look like on the ground? Imagine a room filled with an almost palpable tension, the flicker of candles casting eerie shadows on sacred icons and statues. The priest, clad in a simple but symbolic stole, stands ready, gripping his rosary. The possessed individual may exhibit violent reactions—screaming, thrashing, or speaking in tongues unknown to them. But in the eyes of faith, these are just desperate acts of a malevolent entity losing its grip.

The exorcist continually prays, sometimes for hours or even days, commanding the entity to depart in the name of Jesus Christ. He uses holy water, the crucifix, and relics of saints to aid in the spiritual battle. Every bead of sweat, every whispered prayer, carries the weight of divine authority. It's a war where the weapons are not of this world, and the battlefield is the human soul.

The goals of the exorcism are liberation and healing. Once the demon is expelled, the individual often feels a profound sense of peace and relief, as though a dark cloud has lifted. However, the journey is far from over. Post-exorcism care involves spiritual guidance, ongoing prayer, and often the sacraments, to fortify the individual against any future spiritual attacks.

But why does God allow possession in the first place? It's a perplexing question, one that theologians have debated for centuries. Some argue that possession is a severe form of the trials and tribulations that test our faith. Others believe it serves as a stark reminder of the realities of the spiritual realm, urging the faithful to remain vigilant and devout.

One thing is clear: the Rite of Exorcism is an affirmation of God's ultimate authority over evil. It brings to life the words of St. Paul in Ephesians 6:12, "For we do not wrestle against flesh and blood, but against the rulers, against the authorities, against the powers of this dark world and against the spiritual forces of evil in the heavenly realms." This spiritual confrontation serves as a dramatic, sobering testament to the unseen but ever-present battle between good and evil.

In modern times, the rite has garnered media attention and public interest, sparking curiosity and skepticism alike. However, the sensationalism of Hollywood often overshadows the genuine terror and subsequent liberation experienced by those undergoing the rite. Stories of exorcism remind us that faith, prayer, and the sacraments aren't mere rituals. They are potent, divine tools in the hands of believers.

Exorcism's role in the Church also underscores the importance of living a spiritual life grounded in faith and righteousness. It teaches that we are not merely physical beings but spiritual ones, susceptible to forces that go beyond what the eyes can see. The Church, through exorcism, reiterates its mission to safeguard its flock from harm, both seen and unseen.

The Rite of Exorcism isn't a relic of the past but a vivid declaration of faith's triumph over darkness. It beckons the faithful to witness the gravity of spiritual warfare and the boundless mercy of God. This rite is a clarion call to stand firm in belief, understanding that while evil is real, it's no match for the power of Christ.

While the thought of demonic possession can send chills down one's spine, it's essential to remember that the Church stands as a fortress against such evils. The Rite of Exorcism, with all its dramatic elements, serves as a stark reminder of that divine protection. It's a somber ritual, but one that shines a light on the incredible power of faith and God's unending love for His people.

Notable Exorcists in Church History have long served as the Church's warriors in the shadows, battling supernatural adversaries that most of us only encounter in the pages of Scripture or the dark recesses of our fears. The Church's history is rich with individuals who dedicated their lives to this thankless, dangerous work, displaying faith so steadfast it could move mountains—or, more aptly, banish demons.

One of the most storied exorcists in Church history is St. Benedict of Nursia. Known primarily for founding the Benedictine order and composing the Rule of St. Benedict, his legacy also includes numerous accounts of exorcisms. St. Benedict was known for his deep devotion and strict adherence to prayer and asceticism. His battles with demonic forces were legendary. It's said that he could make evil spirits flee merely by the sign of the cross or a whispered prayer. These stories serve to remind us that holiness and spiritual strength are our most potent weapons.

St. Francis of Assisi, a saint beloved for his gentleness and affinity with nature, also faced demonic adversaries. Though his life was defined by humility and peace, he was no stranger to spiritual warfare. One noted incident involves a man possessed by a demon that St. Francis encountered. The saint approached the man with kindness and courage, and through his prayers, the afflicted individual was delivered from the demonic torment. Such accounts reveal that even the most serene saints wield formidable spiritual strength.

Venturing into more recent history, we find the formidable figure of St. Pio of Pietrelcina, more commonly known as Padre Pio. Famous for bearing the stigmata and his profound piety, Padre Pio also garnered a reputation as a mighty exorcist. Witnesses recount his fierce encounters with demonic forces, where his very presence seemed to torment them. "They torment me," he once said, "But I consider it a good sign." These words highlight a profound truth: those closest to God often find themselves on the front lines of spiritual warfare.

Now let us not overlook St. John Vianney, the Curé of Ars, whose piety attracted multitudes seeking spiritual guidance and healing. His simple, austere life in the rural village of Ars was constantly disrupted by aggressive demonic attacks, which he called 'le grappin,' or the 'grappling hook.' The more he preached and administered sacraments, the more violent the attacks became. Yet, he never wavered. His strength in the face of unrelenting opposition offers an inspiring lesson in persistence and faith. The adversary's fury is, after all, a testament to the effectiveness of our holy endeavors.

Another extraordinary figure in the annals of exorcism is Father Gabriele Amorth. Founder of the International Association of Exorcists and one of the most prolific exorcists of the 20th and 21st centuries, Father Amorth served as the chief exorcist of Rome. He conducted tens of thousands of exorcisms over his lifetime. His book, "An Exorcist Tells His Story," remains a compelling mix of documentation and inspiration. He faced the doubters and skeptics within and outside the Church with a blend of humor and fortitude. His undying commitment to his mission and his fearlessness in the face of evil is a modern-day beacon for the faithful.

These notable exorcists shared common traits: unwavering faith, steadfast courage, and profound humility. They entered spiritual warfare not for glory but out of a sense of divine mission. St. Teresa of Avila, another powerful spiritual warrior, once remarked, "God alone suffices." This idea permeated the lives of these exorcists. They did not rely on human strength but wholly trusted in God's power, manifest through prayer, sacraments, and absolute surrender to His will.

The lesser-known, yet highly impactful, exorcists like St. Vincent Ferrer also contribute to this compelling narrative. Known for his missionary work and conversion of thousands, St. Vincent was frequently called upon to perform exorcisms. His fervent preaching and deep spiritual life made him a formidable opponent to the forces of darkness. Records tell of his ability to discern possessed individuals in crowds, instantly freeing them through his prayers and thus, bringing many souls back to the path of righteousness.

However, not all tales of exorcists are swathed in solemnity. Some instances even carry a hint of divine humor amidst the horror. Consider the life of St. Philip Neri, who is often remembered for his joyful spirit and playful personality. St. Philip had an encounter where his joyous humor disarmed a demonic presence. It's a stark reminder that joy and laughter, too, carry divine power capable of unsettling evil.

The role of exorcists within the Church isn't confined to confronting demons directly. Figures such as St. Ignatius of Loyola, founder of the Jesuits, have shaped spiritual understanding and armed the faithful with spiritual exercises to resist temptation and evil influences. While not documented extensively as an exorcist in the traditional sense, his contributions to spiritual warfare through his teachings are immeasurable, promoting a disciplined interior life that naturally repels evil.

It's essential to recognize the supportive roles that other less-celebrated clergy and lay persons have played in the domain of exorcism. Their contributions, often unrecorded and unnoticed, have been instrumental in the Church's battle against darkness. Monastics, often secluded and forgotten, dedicated lifetimes of prayer for the protection and deliverance of souls. The mystics, with their profound interior insights and spiritual sacrifices, supported the mission of exorcists indirectly yet powerfully.

The Church's long history in exorcism serves as a vibrant testament to the enduring belief in spiritual warfare. These exorcists' lives, filled with both divine encounters and tremendous personal trials, offer a mirror for us today. Their valor and unwavering commitment to God encourage us to persevere in our faith, confront our own spiritual battles with courage, and support each other in the face of adversity.

In conclusion, the saints and holy figures who have performed exorcisms throughout history are more than legends from ancient tomes. They serve as dynamic examples, guiding us in understanding that the struggle against evil is ongoing and multifaceted. Whether through formal rites of exorcism, profound spiritual teachings, or simply living lives of deep faith and devotion, these remarkable individuals remind us that with God's grace, we, too, can stand firm against the darkness.

Exorcism Stories

In the heart of our spiritual battles lie the gripping, often hair-raising stories of exorcism. These modern-day clashes between forces of good and evil would make any thriller seem tame by comparison. Picture the scene: a serene church, a devout priest armed with holy water and prayer, and a tormented soul whose very being is under siege. The sheer intensity of these encounters, where the divine authority confronts malevolent entities, provides a potent reminder of the power of faith. Whether it's the chilling testimony of a possessed individual or the awe-inspiring moment of their deliverance, each story reinforces the unwavering truth that God's power is absolute. These harrowing yet triumphant narratives not only spark a mix of fear and fascination but also serve to embolden the faithful, urging them to lean into their beliefs and stand firm in the righteousness that dispels all darkness.

Real Accounts of Demonic Possession are not merely the fabrications of overactive imaginations or the stuff of Hollywood horror. Far from it. These harrowing tales have been meticulously documented by exorcists who have dedicated their lives to spiritual warfare. One notable figure, Father Gabriele Amorth, who served as the chief exorcist for the Diocese of Rome, has spoken extensively about his chilling encounters with the demonic. His records reveal a world in which evil is palpable, almost tangible, and can be defeated only through unwavering faith and the power granted by God.

Take, for instance, the compelling story of a young girl named Julia (name changed for privacy). Julia was an ordinary teenager, bright and sociable, but her life took a grim turn seemingly out of nowhere. She began to exhibit behavior that was far beyond adolescent angst. Family members noticed her speaking in languages she had never learned, and her voice would shift to an unsettlingly deep tone that was not her own. Objects would fly across the room, and a disturbing darkness seemed to cling to her. Her parents, devout Catholics, were quick to recognize these signs and sought the aid of a local priest who specialized in exorcisms.

Father Michael, the exorcist in this case, described the process as grueling. Julia would thrash violently during the exorcisms, revealing strength inconceivable for her slight frame. Holy water sizzled on her skin, and her eyes would often roll back, showing only the whites—an image that still haunts those who witnessed it. Yet, through persistent prayer and multiple sessions of the Rite of Exorcism, Father Michael ultimately triumphed. Julia's liberation reinforced the family's faith and served as a manifestation of God's power over evil.

Another poignant account comes from the Philippines, involving a man named Carlos. Carlos was a sailor who found himself led astray by various temptations of the flesh while away at sea. Dabbling in occult practices, he unwittingly opened a door to demonic influence. Returning home, Carlos experienced terrifying nocturnal attacks—an invisible force would paralyze him, leaving him breathless as dark whispers filled his ears. Unable to sleep or find peace, Carlos sought help from Father Hector, a seasoned exorcist.

What Father Hector uncovered was spine-chilling. Carlos had become host to multiple demonic entities. During the exorcisms, he would convulse violently, bark like a dog, and at times even reveal knowledge of things he had no earthly way of knowing. His recovery was not instant, but after many intense sessions and a full return to his faith, Carlos was finally set free. His story underscores the peril of straying from God's path and the redemptive power of repentance.

We also have the sobering experience of a small town in Italy, where a seemingly tranquil community faced a collective ordeal. It began with Antonio, a local butcher, who started to notice unusual things happening in his shop—meat would spoil inexplicably, and a cold, eerie chill would pervade the air. Soon, other townsfolk reported hearing anguished cries at night, although no one seemed to be in distress. Antonio, feeling his faith deeply shaken, reached out to the local church.

Father Giuseppe responded to Antonio's plea and agreed to perform an exorcism, suspecting a demonic presence. The ritual revealed an entity that had deep roots in the area, potentially anchored by centuries-old sins committed by previous inhabitants. With Father Giuseppe's relentless divine intervention, peace was restored. However, the town was forever changed, as its residents were reminded of the importance of maintaining a collective faith and righteousness.

These stories are just a fragment of countless such experiences documented by exorcists around the world. They serve as a stark reminder of the spiritual battles fought in realms unseen by the naked eye. The Church, in Her wisdom, offers the Rite of Exorcism not only as a tool of liberation but also as a testament to the ultimate triumph of good over evil. The faithful are urged to take these accounts to heart—not as mere folklore, but as real, tangible proof of the continuous struggle between light and darkness.

As Corinthians 10:4-5 tells us, "The weapons we fight with are not the weapons of the world. On the contrary, they have divine power to demolish strongholds." This divine power, harnessed through unwavering faith, prayer, and adherence to God's commandments, is our bulwark against the malevolent forces that seek to devour us. It is this power that exorcists call upon when faced with the terrifying manifestations of demonic possession, and it is this power that ultimately prevails.

Let us turn our attention to perhaps one of the most documented and spine-tingling cases in modern times—the case of Anneliese Michel in Germany. Anneliese was a young, devout Catholic who began experiencing inexplicable symptoms in her teenage years. She underwent extensive medical treatment but found no relief. Her situation deteriorated rapidly—she would fly into violent rages, contort her body in unnatural ways, and exhibit an aversion to sacred objects and places. It became abundantly clear to her family and her clergy that only a spiritual intervention could save her.

Father Ernst Alt and Father Arnold Renz were called upon to conduct the exorcisms—67 in total. The sessions were heartbreaking and horrific, revealing the presence of multiple demonic entities. Anneliese herself spoke in several different voices, some ancient, some ominously childlike. Her faith and the faith of those around her were tested to their limits. Despite the eventual tragic outcome, her case remains a powerful testament to the reality of demonic possession and the importance of spiritual vigilance.

In closing, these real accounts of demonic possession underscore a fundamental truth echoed throughout the ages and across cultures: evil is real, it is palpable, and it is a force that can only be countered by faith, prayer, and divine intervention. While these stories may incite fear, they also inspire courage and strengthen our resolve. They remind us that our faith is not just a passive belief but an active shield and sword in the spiritual warfare that rages around us. God has equipped us with everything we need to stand firm, resist the devil, and watch him flee.

Triumphs of Deliverance can be both awe-inspiring and terrifying. Imagine the sheer, visceral reality of good clashing with evil, the divine waging war against the demonic forces. Stories of deliverance often read like a battlefield report from a spiritual war where every conceivable strategy is deployed to reclaim a lost soul. It's in these epic confrontations that we witness the sheer power of faith in its most raw form.

Take, for instance, the story of a young woman, hopelessly entangled in the grip of demonic possession. Every moment of her existence was a torment, her nights filled with terrifying nightmares, and her days punctuated by inexplicable fits of rage. But in one decisive battle, an exorcist armed with nothing more than holy water, a crucifix, and fervent prayers, waged a fierce encounter against the malevolent force that had taken hold of her. The struggle was harrowing, the tension palpable, but in the end, the demon was cast out. This wasn't merely a victory; it was a triumph of deliverance, a testament to the boundless power of God's love and mercy. The moment the foul spirit departed, she felt a peace she had long since forgotten, a divine tranquility that filled her heart with profound gratitude.

These stories are not relics of a superstitious past but living testimonies of divine intervention. The Church has documented numerous accounts where exorcists, unyielding in their faith, have confronted darkness head-on and emerged victorious. One might expect these tales to be steeped in endless solemnity, but you'd be surprised how often humor finds its way into even the darkest of battles. Humor becomes a weapon in this spiritual warfare, disarming the adversary and bolstering the spirits of the faithful. Father Amorth, one of the most famous exorcists, often recounted stories with a twinkle in his eye. He would speak of how the Devil, when faced with the resolute faith of the exorcist, would resort to feeble and almost comical attempts to intimidate. Such anecdotes remind us that no matter how terrifying the adversary, the power of Christ renders the devil's antics almost farcical.

In another harrowing yet ultimately uplifting account, a family plagued by incessant and bizarre occurrences sought the help of the church. Furniture moved on its own, whispers filled the night, and an overwhelming sense of dread gnawed at them. The exorcist called in for this daunting task was ready to match wits with whatever malignant force dared to unsettle this family. After days of intense prayer, rituals, and an unwavering stand against evil, the house was finally cleansed. The atmosphere lifted as if a suffocating, dark cloud had been swept away, leaving the family to bask in the newfound peace. The joy and relief on their faces bore light to the triumph of deliverance.

What about the time when a stubborn skeptic found himself reluctantly part of a deliverance that would shake the very core of his disbelief? He scoffed at the very idea of exorcism, convinced it was all hocus-pocus. But circumstances led him to witness an exorcism, and the subsequent transformation of the possessed shattered his doubts. Watching a person restored, seeing the shackles of demonic influence broken, was a visceral experience that left no room for skepticism. In the course of this deliverance, he found himself not only a witness to God's triumph over evil but also to his own conversion of heart. These triumphs capture the essence of faith's power to turn even the most hardened hearts towards God.

Let us not forget that these deliverances also serve to revive the faith of the faithful. They stand as living proof that evil may have its moments of power, but it is inherently doomed to defeat in the face of righteous persistence. These accounts circulate within communities, reigniting a fire of faith, a palpable sense of God's ever-active presence in our lives. They remind us of the promises Christ made and His ultimate victory over sin and death.

The psychological toll on the exorcists themselves is not to be overlooked. These warriors of faith face unimaginable horrors, their resolve tested at every turn. Yet, it is their unwavering belief in God's omnipotence that sees them through. Many of them recount the moments of triumph not with personal pride but with humble gratitude to God for using them as instruments of His will. They are acutely aware that their victories are not theirs alone but shared with the One who gives them strength. An exorcist once explained that the greatest triumph isn't in vanquishing the demon but in witnessing the liberated soul's return to God's grace. It's a reminder that even in the supernatural theater of war, it is the humble, repentant heart that truly glorifies God.

Consider, for a moment, the spiritual ramifications of these triumphs. They serve as stark reminders of the eternal battle between good and evil, urging us to fortify our defenses through prayer, sacraments, and unwavering faith. When we hear of these extraordinary deliverances, we're prompted to look within and ask ourselves if we're properly equipped for our spiritual battles.

They inspire us to cling to our faith, to seek God's grace fervently, and to trust in His providential guidance and protection.

We might also ponder the perspective of the delivered. Emerging from the dark abyss of possession isn't just a return to normalcy; it's an awakening to a life teeming with spiritual vitality. Those who've been delivered often share stories of newfound fervor in their spiritual practices, a deeper appreciation for the sacraments, and an unshakeable commitment to live out their faith boldly and joyfully. Their testimonies act as powerful catalysts for our own spiritual awakening, urging us to strive for a more intimate relationship with God.

In the grand drama of human existence, where every soul is a battleground, these triumphs of deliverance are unmistakable beacons of hope. They are affirmations that even in the darkest of times, the light of God's love can pierce through, bringing redemption and peace. They call us to celebrate God's victories, to lift our hearts in gratitude, and to renew our commitment to live as faithful warriors in Christ's army.

When viewed from the broader tapestry of faith, these triumphs remind us of the ultimate deliverance promised to each of us. Just as the afflicted find solace and freedom through the Church's ministry, so too are we called to seek our deliverance from the sins and trials that beset us. The path of righteousness, though fraught with challenges, is laid out before us, beckoning us to walk it with courage and faith.

We find strength in the truth that no matter how fierce the battle, no matter how dark the night, God's love and power are infinitely greater. The triumphs of deliverance, these stories of God's mighty hand actively working in our world, become our spiritual rallying cry. They leave an indelible mark on our hearts, compelling us to embrace our faith more fully, to cherish the sacraments more deeply, and to trust in God's

Chapter 5: Aphorisms and Teachings

Amidst the cacophony of a world that often feels disjointed and aimless, the timeless aphorisms and teachings of the saints offer a symphony of divine clarity and purpose. St. Augustine calls us to restless pursuit, whispering that our hearts remain unsatisfied until they rest in God, while St. Teresa of Avila tilts her head with a knowing smile, reminding us that patience attains everything. These pearls of wisdom are not mere relics of a bygone era but living, breathing lamp posts, lighting the path to righteousness. Even in the murky waters of despair, the proverbs and sayings from the Bible emerge as lifelines, anchoring our souls with unyielding truth. They invite us to laugh at the absurdity of our own insignificant worries, to shudder at the awesomeness of divine justice, and to rise, again and again, with the hopeful conviction that our battles are never fought alone. To embrace these teachings is to arm oneself with a shield of faith, a weapon forged in heavenly wisdom, and a guide through the labyrinthine corridors of life.

Pearls of Wisdom from Saints

In the labyrinth of life's trials and tribulations, the pearls of wisdom from saints stand as timeless beacons of light. These saintly aphorisms and teachings, bursting with profound insight and divine humor, guide the faithful through treacherous waters and into the safe harbors of spiritual enlightenment. St. Augustine's reflections remind us that "our hearts are restless until they rest in You," while St. Teresa of Avila's counsel, "let nothing disturb you," speaks volumes about the peace that comes from unwavering faith. Such wisdom doesn't merely educate; it galvanizes and terrifies, invoking both a laughter that lifts the soul and a fear of God that redirects our earthly wanderings. The saints, paradoxical carriers of both joy and forewarning, offer morsels of divine truth that beckon every seeker toward eternal righteousness and infinite wisdom.

St. Augustine's Insights are a cornerstone for anyone embarking on the journey of faith, seeking truth, and aiming to tread the path of righteousness. Renowned for his profound and transformative teachings, St. Augustine of Hippo offers a treasure trove of wisdom that continues to inspire, challenge, and guide the faithful. His insights delve deep into the intricacies of the human soul, the nature of God, and the power of grace, all while interweaving a tapestry of humor, sharp wit, and a disarming candor. Let's explore his insights further, not as relics of a distant past but as vibrant, living truths that speak directly to us today.

St. Augustine famously said, "Our hearts are restless until they rest in You, O Lord." In this simple yet profound declaration, he identifies the universal human yearning for divine communion. This restlessness, far from being a curse, is a divine spark urging us towards greater truths and deeper relationships. It's that gnawing emptiness which no earthly delights can fill. We've all sought solace in distractions, be it material wealth, fleeting pleasures, or even misguided pursuits of power. Yet, Augustine's insight urges us to look beyond these transient enticements and seek the eternal fountain of peace in God.

Humor, amidst his spiritual musings, finds a place in Augustine's reflections. In his "Confessions," he recounts the lighter moments of his youth with a twinkle in his eye, from stealing pears just for the thrill to his adolescent follies. By acknowledging his own imperfections with a sense of humor, Augustine invites us to do the same. This humility is not self-deprecation; rather, it is a recognition of our shared human condition. We stumble, we err, but there's always the opportunity for redemption. His humor is a gentle reminder that while we strive for holiness, we're still human, prone to missteps and in need of divine mercy and grace.

Augustine's journey to faith wasn't straightforward. This is perhaps one of the most compelling aspects of his life. He dabbled in Manichaeism, questioned the very essence of truth, and was deeply entangled in earthly desires. Yet he persevered. His mother's continuous prayers and his intellectual quest led him back to the Christian faith. This journey showcases the relentless pursuit of God's truth and serves as a testimony to the power of hope and perseverance. The ups and downs of his spiritual journey remind us that the path to God is often winding, filled with doubts and reconsiderations. But it's through this arduous journey that our faith truly becomes robust and unshakeable.

In "The City of God," Augustine delves into the cosmic struggle between good and evil, illuminating the complexities of moral choices. He sees history itself as a battleground where the City of God and the City of Man perpetually clash. Yet, he doesn't leave us mired in despair. His insights are uplifting, reminding us that divine providence guides us even amidst chaos. He challenges us to rise above earthly conflicts and align ourselves with divine purpose. But make no mistake, Augustine's depictions of evil are harrowing, a stark reminder that the forces of darkness are real and ever-present. However, the promise of salvation and the triumph of God offer a beacon of hope.

His reflections on grace are particularly moving. Augustine was a staunch advocate of the necessity of divine grace for salvation. He poignantly wrote, "God loves each of us as if there were only one of us." Every soul is precious, unique, and thoughtfully crafted by God. Grace, for Augustine, is not just a gift but an essential lifeline that sustains and transforms. This unsparing love of God, which reaches out to us despite our failings, carries a dual message of comfort and a call to action. We are comforted knowing that we are infinitely loved, and we are called to let that grace mold us into reflections of divine love and mercy in our world.

One of the most chilling, yet captivating, aspects of Augustine's writings is his exploration of the nature of sin and its consequences. He doesn't sugarcoat the grim realities of a life steeped in sin. His depictions of the sins of the flesh, pride, and false idols are stark and vivid. Yet in the same breath, he balances horror with the hope of repentance. He asserts, "There is no saint without a past, no sinner without a future." This reminder is both a profound warning and an invitation to transform. It tells us that while the consequences of sin are real and often terrifying, redemption is always within reach if we turn our hearts back to God.

In addressing the intellectual side of faith, Augustine's works, like "On Christian Doctrine," dissect the principles of biblical exegesis and the role of reason. He masterfully marries faith and reason, showing that they are not opposing forces but complementary. For him, the search for wisdom is a delight and a passion, an endless pursuit that brings one closer to God. His teachings underscore that knowledge and faith go hand in hand, with the former enhancing the latter. The intellectual journey through Augustine's insights is a thrilling adventure, rife with discoveries that challenge the mind and elevate the soul.

St. Augustine's musings on time and eternity are another profound aspect of his insights. His assertion that time is a creation of God and that eternity is God's own realm invite us to ponder our own finite existence. Augustine postulates that past, present, and future are constructs of a temporal world, whereas God exists beyond these bounds. This challenges us to view our lives not as a series of chronological events but as a continuum that's deeply rooted in eternity. Such a perspective can be unsettling, yet it's profoundly inspirational, urging us to transcend temporal anxieties and align our lives with the eternal purposes of God.

For those struggling with the weight of guilt, Augustine's narrative offers a balm of forgiveness and renewal. His own life—marked by moments of profound regret and eventual repentance—serves as a testament to the transformative power of God's love. He assures us that no sin is too great to be forgiven if the heart sincerely seeks God.

This message is particularly poignant for those who feel trapped by their past. Augustine reassures us through his own example that repentance isn't just about feeling sorry for one's sins; it's about a complete turning away from them and allowing God's grace to work its miracle of transformation.

In summary, the wealth of St. Augustine's insights offers a multifaceted approach to understanding faith, human existence, and our eternal destiny. Through humor and motivation, horror, and profound theology, Augustine leads us through a labyrinth of thought that reveals the heart of Christian doctrine and the soul's journey towards God. His writings are not just relics of religious scholarship but living texts, brimming with life, and full of relevance for today's faithful. They beckon us to dive deep into the mysteries of faith, to laugh at our human follies, to shudder at the realities of sin, and ultimately to be uplifted by the promise of God's redeeming love.

St. Teresa of Avila's Teachings transcend time, offering profound insights into the spiritual path and divine union. A mystic, a reformer, and a Doctor of the Church, St. Teresa's teachings guide the faithful through the mysterious and often arduous path to spiritual enlightenment. Her wisdom, gleaned from profound personal experiences and divine revelations, serves as both a beacon and a mirror for those seeking the face of God.

One of St. Teresa's central teachings is the importance of interior prayer, which she describes in her seminal work, "The Interior Castle." She depicts the soul as a castle made of a single diamond, encompassing numerous rooms that represent various stages of spiritual development. The journey inward, through meditation and prayer, leads one closer to the innermost chamber where God resides. Here, we find not only the divine but also our true selves, purified and prepared for union with God. This process is neither swift nor simple, often requiring perseverance and divine grace, but the reward, as Teresa assures, is beyond mortal comprehension.

In a world obsessed with external achievements and distractions, Teresa's emphasis on contemplative prayer is a stark reminder of where true treasure lies. She encourages believers to engage in "mental prayer," a form of prayer that goes beyond vocal recitation to a deeper meditation and communication with God. It's a method that invites one into a personalized, intimate relationship with the divine, offering solace, guidance, and peace amidst life's chaos.

Another critical aspect of St. Teresa's teachings is her focus on humility. In her view, humility is the foundation of all virtues, essential for spiritual progress. Teresa herself exemplified this through her reforms of the Carmelite order, where she faced fierce opposition and hardships. Her humility was not of servility but of strength and grace, recognizing her limitations and placing her unwavering trust in God. She famously said, "Humility, humility. It is the virtue I love most. If you consider how highly it is esteemed by Him who is our one model, you will be content with little exertion if undertaken for Him."

Despite the awe-inspiring nature of her sanctity, Teresa's teachings are remarkably accessible and pragmatic. She advises on everyday struggles, noting that spiritual life does not demand extraordinary experiences but a dedication to small acts of love and faithfulness. Her humor often shines through in her writings, making her relatable and her teachings easier to embrace. One of her well-known quotes, "God save us from gloomy saints," highlights her belief that a joyful heart is fundamental to the Christian life.

St. Teresa also underscores the significance of community. While personal prayer and contemplation are vital, she understood the necessity of communal support and guidance. Her efforts in reforming the Carmelite convents were aimed at creating spaces where sincerity, simplicity, and shared devotion could flourish. She believed that spiritual growth is often catalyzed by the example and support of others walking the same path.

One of the more frightening elements of Teresa's teachings is her vivid descriptions of spiritual trials and the reality of demonic oppression. She does not shy away from discussing the darkness that can assail the soul. In "The Life of Teresa of Jesus," she writes extensively about her own bouts with demonic forces, providing both a caution and a testament to God's ultimate power over evil. Teresa teaches that these trials, though terrifying, serve to purify and strengthen the soul, reinforcing the necessity of unwavering faith and trust in God.

Importantly, St. Teresa's teachings resonate deeply with the concepts of love and divine intimacy. She frequently refers to God as her "Beloved" and describes her mystical experiences as moments of profound spiritual marriage. This imagery serves to illustrate the depth of intimacy and love that God offers to those who seek Him earnestly. It's a love that not only comforts and sustains but also transforms, leading the soul to transcendent heights of spiritual union.

In her final moments, Teresa's life and teachings coalesce into a singular testament to God's enduring presence and grace. Her last words, "My Lord, it is time to move on. Well then, may your will be done. O my Lord and my Spouse, the hour that I have longed for has come," capture the essence of her lifelong devotion and intimate relationship with God. They stand as a call to all believers to embrace their own spiritual journeys with courage and faith, always seeking the face of the Divine amidst life's trials and tribulations.

Proverbs and Sayings from the Bible

The Bible, full of divine wisdom, offers a treasury of proverbs and sayings that resonate through the ages. These timeless pieces of wisdom connect the hearts of the faithful to the very core of divine truth. They aren't just lofty ideas; they are practical guides, moral compasses, and a source of daily inspiration. Take, for example, the simple yet profound admonition from Proverbs 3:5-6, "Trust in the Lord with all your heart and lean not on your own understanding; in all your ways submit to him, and he will make your paths straight." It's not just a call to faith but a roadmap for living a life of trust and obedience.

One cannot overlook the striking contrast often presented between the righteous and the wicked in these proverbs. Proverbs 4:18-19 starkly declares, "The path of the righteous is like the morning sun, shining ever brighter till the full light of day. But the way of the wicked is like deep darkness; they do not know what makes them stumble." Here, the Bible deftly paints a vivid picture of the effectiveness and consequences of one's choices, reminding believers of the light that comes from walking in God's ways and the confusion that ensues from straying from His path.

The humor in the Bible is subtle but definitely present, often embedded in its pearls of wisdom. Like in Proverbs 21:9, "Better to live on a corner of the roof than share a house with a quarrelsome wife." It presents an amusing yet pointed reminder of the importance of harmony and peace within the household, which is something every Roman Catholic family strives for.

The beauty of biblical proverbs lies in their relatability and their applicability to our everyday lives. Proverbs 27:17 states, "As iron sharpens iron, so one person sharpens another." This is an invocation for community and fellowship, encouraging the faithful to support, challenge, and uplift one another, particularly during times of spiritual struggle. This pushes us to reflect on our own relationships, nudging us towards being better friends, family members, and lay ministers.

Some sayings evoke a sense of horror and fear, meant to kindle the fear of God in the hearts of sinners. Proverbs 6:16-19 lists the seven deadly sins, and it's anything but comforting: "There are six things the Lord hates, seven that are detestable to him: haughty eyes, a lying tongue, hands that shed innocent blood, a heart that devises wicked schemes, feet that are quick to rush into evil, a false witness who pours out lies, and a person who stirs up conflict in the community." This stark list serves as a jarring wake-up call to those entertaining thoughts of sin, urging an immediate realignment towards righteousness.

For those searching for clear guidance, the Bible doesn't disappoint. Proverbs 1:7 succinctly lays out the foundation for wisdom: "The fear of the Lord is the beginning of knowledge, but fools despise wisdom and instruction." This is the entry point for any seeker of truth and understanding, emphasizing that humility and reverence for God open the door to divine wisdom.

Balance is key in many of these proverbs. Take Proverbs 20:28 for instance, "Love and faithfulness keep a king safe; through love his throne is made secure." This illustrates that strength and authority are grounded in virtues such as love and faithfulness. These virtues are not just meant for kings but for anyone in a position of leadership or responsibility.

Proverbs also lay the groundwork for social justice and ethical living. Proverbs 14:31 says, "Whoever oppresses the poor shows contempt for their Maker, but whoever is kind to the needy honors God." This doesn't just fully endorse charity; it ties our treatment of the less fortunate directly to our relationship with God. How we treat the marginalized and oppressed is a direct reflection of our reverence for the Divine Creator.

The playful humor of Proverbs can also be seen in sayings like Proverbs 26:11, "As a dog returns to its vomit, so fools repeat their folly." The image here is intentionally vivid, almost grotesque, to underline the stupidity of repeating the same mistakes. It's a call to learn from our errors rather than stubbornly sticking to our ways.

Conversely, sayings such as Proverbs 16:32 offer a motivational and inspirational push towards self-control and patience: "Better a patient person than a warrior, one with self-control than one who takes a city." It's a majestic exaltation of inner strength over brute force, celebrating the quiet power of patience.

Many proverbs are just plain practical. Proverbs 27:1 advises, "Do not boast about tomorrow, for you do not know what a day may bring." This is both a reminder to live in the present and an endorsement of humility, traits that are invaluable in leading a spiritually fulfilling life.

There's something immortally endearing about Proverbs 17:22 as well, "A cheerful heart is good medicine, but a crushed spirit dries up the bones." Here, humor and joy are valued not just as pleasant emotions but as essential components of a healthy, godly life.

But to really place the fear of God in our hearts, Proverbs 11:21 says it all, "Be sure of this: The wicked will not go unpunished, but those who are righteous will go free." This speaks directly to divine justice, a sobering reminder that our actions bear eternal consequences and that God's judgment is always fair.

The proverbs of the Bible, sometimes conciliatory, sometimes stern, and often sprinkled with humor, serve as inexhaustible springs of wisdom. For Roman Catholics, these sayings aren't just ancient words on a page; they're living, breathing guides that lead us closer to God's own heart.

Chapter 6: The Transformative Power of Repentance

Repentance, a word seemingly whispered with the weight of ages, holds the extraordinary power to transform lives and lead souls back to the grace of God. Imagine the moment of St. Paul's dramatic conversion, when a man once known for persecuting Christians encountered the divine and was set on an entirely new path. Or consider the story of St. Mary Magdalene, who shed her past sins through sincere contrition and became a devoted follower of Christ. These are not ancient tales relegated to dusty scrolls but living testimonies that echo into our present, urging us to confront our own transgressions and seek reconciliation. Today, the call to repentance is as urgent as ever; it's not merely an acknowledgment of our faults but a profound transformation of the heart. It's like a spiritual rejuvenation, cutting through the banality of daily life with the precision of a surgeon's scalpel, extracting sin and replacing it with the life-giving grace of forgiveness.

Repentance, when embraced wholly, kindles the spark of divine renewal within us, setting our spirits ablaze with a fervor for goodness and a hunger for the truth.

Stories of Conversion

In the shadow of their darkest hours, when hope seemed a faint whisper and sin's grip relentless, many have found an astonishing transformation through repentance. Consider St. Paul, who, from his notorious persecution of Christians, encountered the blinding light on the road to Damascus, reshaping his soul from ruthless oppressor to fervent apostle of Christ. Then, there's the tale of St. Mary Magdalene, deemed a lost cause by many, yet through her sincere repentance, she washed the feet of Jesus with her tears and became a pillar of unwavering faith. These stories, blending tragedy and redemption, illuminate the awe-inspiring power of repentance. They remind us that no matter the abyss one has plunged into, the path of humility and genuine contrition can lift the soul to divine heights, sparking a new life bathed in grace and wisdom.

St. Paul's Dramatic Conversion, a tale of divine intervention that shakes us to the core, holds within it the power to awaken the most hardened hearts and enliven our spirits. Picture a man consumed by fervent hate, intent on stamping out the burgeoning faith of the early Christians. That man was Saul of Tarsus. His mission? To persecute and obliterate the followers of Christ. Little did he know, his journey to Damascus would be his spiritual crucible, reshaping his soul in ways unfathomable to even the most imaginative minds.

Saul was no ordinary zealot. He was a Roman citizen, educated under the esteemed Gamaliel and zealous for the traditions of his ancestors. Yet, this was a zeal misdirected—a fervor that turned murderous. With each step towards Damascus, he carried letters authorizing the capture and imprisonment of Christians. His heart was set on destruction, his intent as steely as his resolve. But Divine Providence had other plans.

As the sun blazed overhead, a light more brilliant than any Saul had ever seen suddenly surrounded him. Falling to the ground, he heard a voice, firm yet compassionate: "Saul, Saul, why do you persecute me?" With eyes wide but seeing nothing, Saul asked, "Who are you, Lord?" The voice replied, "I am Jesus, whom you are persecuting." Trembling and astonished, Saul found himself helpless, blinded by the encounter.

Through this moment, the mighty hand of God revealed Himself not in wrath but in redirection. The terror Saul felt—face down in the dust, blinded and bewildered—was but the first step in a profound transformation. The once fiery persecutor was led, humbled and vulnerable, into Damascus. For three days, he neither ate nor drank, engulfed in total darkness. This was not just physical blindness; it was a darkness of the soul, waiting to be flooded with divine light.

It was in this period of utter darkness that God sent Ananias, a devout disciple, to find Saul. Despite his initial fear—after all, Saul's reputation as a persecutor preceded him—Ananias obeyed the divine command.

Placing his hands on Saul, he declared, "Brother Saul, the Lord—Jesus, who appeared to you on the road as you were coming here—has sent me so that you may see again and be filled with the Holy Spirit." Immediately, something like scales fell from Saul's eyes, and his sight was restored.

The scales falling from Saul's eyes were symbolic of the veil lifting from his soul, revealing the profound truth of Christ's love and sacrifice. He rose, was baptized, and took food, regaining his strength. Saul, now Paul, would no longer be a persecutor of Christians but a fervent apostle of Christ. This is the heart of true conversion: a complete and radical transformation, not merely of the mind, but of the heart and soul.

Let's imagine what it must have been like for the early Christians who witnessed this change. The terror that Saul once instilled in their hearts now turned into amazement and burgeoning hope. Paul's conversion was not just a personal transformation; it was a divine declaration of mercy, an example of

God's infinite capacity to redeem even the most unlikely souls.

Paul's newfound mission was fraught with peril and opposition. Imagine being doubted and distrusted by those you now sought to join, your past haunting every step you took. Yet, fueled by an unquenchable fire within, Paul preached boldly, with a fervor surpassing even his former zeal. His dramatic transformation became a cornerstone of his ministry: if Paul, the chief persecutor, could be saved, what excuse could others possibly have for resisting God's call?

To many, Paul's letters to the early Christian communities are a testament to a life wholly surrendered to Christ. "For to me, to live is Christ and to die is gain," he wrote to the Philippians, capturing the essence of his radical conversion. He counted all things as loss compared to the surpassing worth of knowing Christ Jesus his Lord. The fear of God had been planted firmly within him, yet it blossomed into a profound love and dedication.

Paul's journey reminds us that no one is beyond the reach of divine grace. It serves as both a warning and an inspiration—warning us about the dangers of zeal without true understanding and inspiring us by showing that God's grace can unlock even the most impenetrable hearts. The horror of his initial persecution is eclipsed only by the awe of his transformative experience.

It is easy to dismiss the story of St. Paul's conversion as just another biblical tale, but its implications go far beyond the pages of sacred scripture. Each of us, in our struggles and wayward paths, can see a reflection of Saul's obstinate heart. We may not be persecutors, but we all resist God's will in our ways. Paul's conversion is an everlasting reminder that our journey doesn't end with our sins. Redemption and transformation are always within our reach, no matter how lost we may feel.

What did Paul gain through this radical shift? He gained Christ, and with Christ, a mission to spread hope and truth to all corners of the world. His letters, filled with wisdom and fervent exhortations, continue to guide and inspire us. Consider how many hearts have been moved by his words, how many have found courage in his journey. Paul's life serves as a beacon, illustrating that God's power is made perfect in our weakness.

As Paul himself would later write, "If God is for us, who can be against us?" This rhetorical question, brimming with assurance and challenge, echoes the relentless hope found in his conversion. It urges us to consider our battles, our failings, and realize that with God, transformation is not just possible—it's inevitable.

Thus, St. Paul's dramatic conversion stands as a powerful testament to God's infinite mercy and transformative power. It is an invitation to each of us, especially those wandering in the wilderness of doubt and sin. God calls us, just as He called Paul, to leave behind our former ways and embrace a new path of righteousness and wisdom. Let Paul's journey be a signpost on your own road of conversion, a reminder that no matter how

dark the night, the dawn of God's grace is
ever at hand.

St. Mary Magdalene's Redemption is a tale as complex as it is inspiring, a story of immense transformation that transcends time and touches the very soul of the faithful. Mary Magdalene, often mistakenly caricatured solely as a repentant sinner, is instead a living tapestry of grace, courage, and spiritual rebirth.

Here was a woman vilified by her past, overshadowed by her sins, yet destined to become a beacon of redemption. The Gospels tell us that Jesus cast seven demons out of her, marking a pivotal moment in her life. Imagine the horror and anguish of being possessed, stripped of your will and dignity, only to be saved by a touch that dispelled darkness like the dawn. One can almost hear her silent cry for liberation, one that didn't just reach the ears but pierced the very heart of Christ.

Her story doesn't end in deliverance; it begins there. Released from the chains of her past, Mary Magdalene became a staunch follower of Jesus, embodying the unwavering faith we're all called to. She was present at the Crucifixion, and, in a moment drenched in both sorrow and divine revelation, she became the first witness to the Resurrection. Can there be a more profound symbol of redemption than to be chosen as the harbinger of Christ's victory over death?

The depth of her transformation serves as a potent reminder that no one is beyond the reach of God's mercy. She transitioned from a life of torment to one of the most intimate encounters with the divine. And isn't that the very essence of our faith? To believe that no matter how mired we are in sin, redemption is but a confession and repentance away, achievable through the boundless grace of God.

Interestingly, Mary's role wasn't merely passive. Her actions post-redemption resonate with lessons in courage and evangelization. She brought the news of the Resurrection to the apostles, a mission fraught with doubt and the risk of disbelief. Yet, her testimony paved the way for the apostles to witness the empty tomb themselves. In this, Mary stands as a paragon of steadfast testimony, urging us to bear witness to our faith despite the world's scepticism.

The horror of her demonic possession gives way to the motivational crescendo of her redemption. Those early, dark moments of her life add weight and significance to her later role. It's as if the darker the night, the brighter the dawn that follows. This oscillation between despair and salvation creates a narrative tension that is both terrifying and sublime, urging believers to see the weight of sin and the power of divine forgiveness.

In redeeming Mary Magdalene, Christ didn't just save a soul; He unveiled the promise of universal grace. He demonstrated that His mercy knows no bounds, extending it to one from whom society had turned away. This act should enkindle hope within us, fanning the flames of courage to seek forgiveness and start anew.

Catholics have always seen Mary Magdalene as a figure of hope and conversion. She's acknowledged in prayers, liturgies, and countless works of art, each iteration capturing a facet of her complex journey. Her feast day on July 22nd is not merely a commemoration but a celebration of redemption—ours and hers.

You might say that the very bones of her story are humorous in the stark contrast they provide. A public sinner turned saint? It's so improbable that it almost invites a wry smile. But this isn't a quip at divine scriptwriting; it's an invitation to joy, a joyful exclamation mark on the heart-wrenching tale of her soul's odyssey.

Mary's redemption should prod us to reflect on our own lives. What chains do we bear, and who can break them if not Christ? The lesson here isn't cloaked in abstract theology but lived experience. Her transformational arc presents a clear path: acknowledge our sins, seek His mercy, and let His love reenact Easter morning in our lives.

The motivations behind her unwavering dedication after her salvation are layered. Was it gratitude? An unquenchable thirst for divine love? Or the sheer joy of being freed from darkness? Perhaps it was all of these. In her, we see that the fruits of redemption are multifarious—joy, dedication, and an unstoppable zest to follow the path illuminated by Christ Himself.

The takeaways from St. Mary Magdalene's redemption are as extensive as they are profound. Her life remains a powerful sermon on the transformative power of repentance and the inexhaustible mercy of Christ. Let her story inspire us to confront our own demons, to run towards Jesus, and to announce to the world that He is risen, and because He lives, we can face tomorrow.

The Church venerates her not as a footnote in Jesus' ministry but as a vital, radiant testimony to the radical, unending love of God. Her story, a divine comedy with twists of terror and triumph, calls us to remember that salvation is dramatic, deeply personal, and available to all.

Encouraging Repentance Today

Encouraging repentance today might sound like a quaint notion to some, but let's not kid ourselves—it's as vital now as ever. Modern life, with its hustle and constant bombardment of distractions, makes it easy to lose sight of that pivotal act of repentance. Yet, repentance, with its transformative power, is like a spiritual reset button, rejuvenating the soul and redirecting it towards God's love and grace. Picture it as a divine intervention, cutting through the noise, a beacon guiding us back to our true purpose. The stories of conversion from both the Biblical era and modern times illustrate that repentance is not just an ancient ritual but a living practice that continues to change lives.

Consider the tale of St. Paul, a persecutor of Christians who encountered a transformation so profound that it altered the course of Christianity. Or think of Mary Magdalene, a sinner turned saint, whose journey of repentance led her to become a close follower of Christ. These stories underscore the universal truth that repentance offers a second chance, a fresh start, no matter how far one has strayed. If these illustrious examples feel a little grand for your taste, know that everyday people, people like you and me, experience the same type of transformation when they open themselves to repentance.

So, how do we encourage repentance today? First, by making it accessible and relatable. Too often, repentance is wrapped up in archaic language and rituals that seem distant from our daily lives. It's not merely about confessing sins in a confessional booth; it's about nurturing a genuine, heartfelt sorrow for our wrongdoings and a sincere desire to change. To encourage this, our communities need to create spaces where people feel safe to express their struggles without judgment. The Church can become a sanctuary of love and understanding, offering counsel, support, and the much-needed assurance that no one is beyond redemption.

Further, the role of humor and joy mustn't be overlooked. Integrating a lighthearted approach, like the jokes and anecdotes from the lives of saints as seen in later chapters, helps in making the concept of repentance less intimidating. Imagine encouraging someone to look at their imperfections with a sprinkle of humor: "Ah, yes, another sin checked off! If this were a bingo game, I'd have won!" It's not about making light of sin but rather reducing the burden of guilt that can paralyze people from seeking forgiveness.

It's also worth mentioning the horror aspect of ignoring repentance. Real exorcism stories, as covered in a previous chapter, provide chilling reminders of the dark consequences when souls remain unrepentant and vulnerable to evil. While it's not our place to scare people into repentance, the gravity of ignoring it should be transparent. These tales serve a dual purpose—reaffirming the power of God's grace while cautioning against complacency.

To drive repentance home in today's society, it helps to anchor it in relatable, lived experiences. Testimonials from individuals who have undergone personal transformations can be profoundly inspiring. A story shared by someone who has turned their life around can spark the initial curiosity and courage someone else needs to embark on their path to repentance. Hearing a fellow parishioner talk about their journey from darkness to light brings the concept of repentance from the lofty heights of theology down to earth, where it belongs—among the people, in their daily grind.

Repentance isn't just a one-time event, either. It's a continuous process, like tending to a garden that constantly needs weeding, watering, and nurturing. Encourage the faithful to view repentance as an ongoing dialogue with God, a regular act of turning back towards Him. The little acts of contrition we make daily—the silent apologies, the commitment to do better—accumulate to mold us slowly but surely into more compassionate, faithful beings.

Equally essential is fostering an environment where the sacraments are not just seen as rituals but as living encounters with God's mercy. The sacrament of confession, often underutilized and misunderstood, should be re-introduced as a powerful tool for spiritual renewal. Breaking down misconceptions and making the sacrament more approachable can demystify the process. Priests, with their pivotal role, can adopt a pastoral approach that reassures rather than reproves, emphasizing God's boundless mercy over judgment.

Moreover, the impact of our actions on others should be a focal point. Repentance isn't a solitary act but one that has a ripple effect on the community. By choosing to repent and amend our ways, we positively influence those around us. Imagine a workplace where employees see their boss genuinely apologize for a mistake and take corrective actions. This act of humility can foster a culture of accountability, grace, and moral integrity. Similarly, in families, when parents model repentance for their children, it teaches them the value of humility and the power of making amends.

In our digital age, leveraging technology to spread messages of repentance can reach wider audiences. Short video testimonials, podcasts discussing spiritual journeys, and even social media campaigns centred around stories of transformation can break through to those who might never step foot in a church. The internet can be a tool for spiritual growth if used thoughtfully, turning screens from sources of distraction into gateways of grace.

Lastly, prayer remains a cornerstone for nurturing a repentant heart. Encouraging the faithful to incorporate prayers for repentance into their daily routines can keep this practice at the forefront of their spiritual lives. Simple, heartfelt prayers asking for God's forgiveness and guidance can be as transformative as any grand act of contrition.

To summarize, encouraging repentance today involves demystifying and humanizing the act, fostering supportive communities, utilizing humor and horror appropriately, sharing relatable testimonials, integrating it into sacraments, highlighting its communal impact, leveraging technology, and grounding it in prayer. By doing so, we remind ourselves and others that no matter how far we wander, the path back to God's loving embrace is always open, waiting to transform our lives.

Chapter 7: Living a Fulfilling Spiritual Life

How do you live a life so spiritually charged that even the pitfalls of sin flee in terror? The answer lies in intertwining faith with every fiber of your being. Picture a life where every action is an echo of divine love, where prayer and meditation are not mere rituals but a direct hotline to the heavens. Attend Mass not out of obligation but for the electrifying connection to the Holy Sacraments, turning mundane routines into sacred rites. Embrace the sacramentals—those humble yet potent objects imbued with divine blessings—as daily catalysts for grace. This spiritual tapestry you weave, thread by divine thread, fortifies your soul against the lurking shadows, transforming every day into a tapestry of holiness and profound fulfillment. What could be more terrifying to the forces of darkness than a life lived in dazzling, unyielding light?

Daily Practices to Strengthen Faith

To live a fulfilling spiritual life anchored in the Catholic tradition, one must adopt daily practices that reinforce and deepen faith. Start with prayer and meditation; they are not just rituals but conversations with the Divine, tuning your soul to the frequency of grace and wisdom. Make attending Mass and the sacraments a cornerstone of your routine; they are lifelines of spiritual nourishment and channels of God's infinite mercy. Immerse yourself in the Word, letting Biblical teachings guide your everyday actions. Utilize sacramentals like rosaries, medals, and holy water, which serve as constant, tangible reminders of the sacred. These practices become the armor and shield in the great spiritual warfare, fortifying you against the snares of doubt and despair. Engage in acts of charity and love, reflecting Christ's light in a world often cloaked in shadows. Faith, after all, is a journey—a labyrinth filled with both divine encounters and trials that test your spirit. But remember, always walk this path with a heart eager for divine whispers and a spirit resilient against the shadows of doubt.

Prayer and Meditation have always been the lifeblood of the Catholic spiritual journey. You see, engaging in consistent prayer and meditation isn't just a pious requirement; it's a gateway to transformation, a binding thread connecting Heaven and Earth. It's the secret weapon that can slice through the darkness and confusion of modern life, like a celestial sword sparking fires of clarity and purpose in our sometimes mundane existence.

Imagine a world where every moment feels like an encounter with the Divine, where every challenge is an opportunity to draw closer to God's infinite wisdom. That's what prayer and meditation can offer. They're not merely rituals confined to Sunday Mass or moments of crisis. They're lifelines, conduits that connect us to the eternal love and mercy of God. In the chaos of daily life, these practices become sanctuaries of peace, guiding lights in the fog of uncertainty.

Think of St. Francis of Assisi, who found divine wisdom in the simplicity of nature, or St. Therese of Lisieux, who discovered profound meaning in the "little ways" of everyday life. Through prayer and meditation, they transcended their earthly struggles and experienced an intimate union with God. We're not so different from these saints. With the right dedication, even our ordinary lives can be transformed into extraordinary tales of divine encounters.

Prayer is not just talking to God; it's a sacred dialogue, a lifeline in times of despair and a totem of joy in times of abundance. When words fail, meditation steps in as a quiet rebellion against the noise of the world. It's in these quiet moments where souls are whispered secrets by the Divine, where landscapes of wisdom unfold, oftentimes in the most unexpected ways.

But let's not confuse meditation with the popularized, secular versions making rounds today. In its truest Catholic sense, meditation is a deep engagement with the mysteries of faith, often anchored by Scripture, the lives of the saints, or the teachings of the Church. It's a heartfelt reflection that goes beyond mere mindfulness. It's an invitation to dwell in God's presence, to sit at His feet, and to soak in His word.

There's a humor in the human struggle of maintaining a prayer life. Picture this: you're ready for serene communion with God, only to realize your mind has wandered to what's for dinner or tomorrow's tasks. We've all been there, facing the delightful absurdity of our own distractions. Yet, it is precisely this persistent return to prayer, despite interruptions, that fortifies our relationship with God. And believe me, He treasures each attempt, however flawed it might seem to us.

From the terrifying accounts of those who have glimpsed purgatory and hell, like St. Catherine of Genoa, we understand the urgency of prayer for our souls and for the souls in need. Prayer becomes the shield against the horrors of spiritual desolation, a comforting blanket in the face of eternal night. It is both our battle cry and our solace, our call to arms and our peaceful retreat.

In the quiet of the night or the break of dawn, this rhythm of prayer and meditation can transform the rosiest optimist and the staunchest skeptic alike. For those wandering in pursuit of meaning, the ritual of checking in with the Divine brings the clarity of a well-lit path amidst a darkened forest. There's an inherent power in this regularity, transforming randomness into purpose.

A structured approach can make this manageable. Start simple: dedicate specific times each day to prayer and meditation. The beauty of the Rosary is its meditative rhythm, guiding the mind through the life of Christ and the intercession of the Blessed Mother. Or perhaps the Liturgy of the Hours can punctuate your day with pauses for contemplation, aligning your internal clock with the rhythm of God's time.

Feel your soul drift towards complacency? Remember St. Augustine's piercing insight, "Our hearts are restless until they rest in You." It's a rallying cry to delve deeper, to push beyond the surface and engage earnestly with the divine mysteries. The weighty wisdom contained in each utterance, in every silent meditation, is a treasure chest waiting to be unlocked by your devotion.

For centuries, the Church has nurtured various forms of prayer and meditation—from the repetitive solace of chanting psalms to the profound silence of Eucharistic Adoration. Each form has its unique grace, providing a diverse toolkit. Explore these different practices and find what resonates most deeply with your spiritual rhythm.

And let's not forget the joyous transformation that wins the day. Yes, there might be moments of horror and intense spiritual battle—think of the harrowing exorcism stories and demonic possessions that shake the flimsiest foundations of faith. Yet, it's in these bracing encounters where prayer shows its fiercest strength. The triumphs of deliverance are testimonies to prayer's potent power, the ultimate exclamation point declaring victory over darkness.

You see, every prayer is heard, every moment of meditation cherished. Even when we falter, our imperfect attempts are the very steps that lead us towards perfection. It is in our persistence that our souls are refined, and our spirits enlivened. This is the ongoing miracle of prayer and meditation: it transforms not only our lives but the world around us.

So, allow your prayers to be the anchor that holds you steady in stormy seas and your meditations the compass that guides you through uncharted waters. They are not just practices; they are the very essence of a fulfilling spiritual life, leading you straight into the arms of divine wisdom and eternal grace.

Attending Mass and the Sacraments isn't merely a religious obligation, it's an immersion into a narrative of divine love and spiritual rejuvenation. Imagine, if you will, the flow of a river—constant, life-giving, and cleansing. This is the essence of participating in Mass and receiving the sacraments. We journey like wanderers in the desert to the oasis of the Eucharist, where refreshments aren't of water but of the blood and body of Christ.

Picture the early dawn on a Sunday, the church bells calling the faithful. There's something profoundly comforting in this call and response—a summons that echoes not just in the air but in the soul, nudging it toward the sanctuary where the sacred drama of the Mass unfolds. As Flannery O'Connor so aptly noted, if it's just a symbol, then to hell with it. This is no mere ritual; it's a celestial banquet where the ordinary meets the divine.

Often, the beauty of the Mass can be found in its predictability. The rhythm of the prayers, the rise and fall of hymns, and the solemnity of the consecration offer a sacred constancy in an otherwise chaotic world. But don't let this familiarity numb the wonder. Each Mass is a new encounter with the divine, an opportunity to bring your burdens to the altar and leave them there.

Consider the sacraments as milestones on the road to sanctity. Baptism, our initiation into the Christian life, isn't just a rite of passage but a profound transformation—albeit one that leaves the participants squawking more often than not! If there's a horror story of spiritual neglect, it's the tale of one baptized but forgotten, like a seed planted and left without sunlight or water.

Confirmation follows, a sacrament often dismissed as a kind of graduation. But woe to those who treat it lightly! It's the Pentecost of your soul, the moment when the Holy Spirit descends to fortify you for spiritual warfare. Without it, your faith could become a candle in the wind, flickering and at risk of extinction with every gust of doubt.

Then there's Confession, a sacrament wrapped in equal parts dread and relief. Walking into the confessional, you might feel like a sheepish prisoner approaching judgment. Yet, emerging from it feels like a parole granted by divine clemency. The horror lies not in the exposure of our failings but in the risk of carrying their burdens unshriven. Imagine the toll it takes on the soul: a torturous affliction, as real as any physical ailment. And then, the sweet, liberating words, "I absolve you of your sins."

Meanwhile, the Eucharist stands as the pinnacle, the "source and summit" of the Christian life. As the bread becomes body and the wine becomes blood, the cosmic meets the corporal. It's humbling, it's wondrous, and sometimes it's downright terrifying—in the most awe-inspiring way. The priest's hands, lifted in consecration, become instruments of the divine, and we, mere mortals, are invited to partake.

Marriage, that hallowed sacrament, isn't just two people exchanging vows. It's a triune partnership, blessed by the Holy Spirit, reflecting the unbreakable bond between Christ and His Church. It's a battlefield and a sanctuary, where love conquers all and in the same breath, is tested by fire. How else could you describe this paradox where the most profound love requires the deepest sacrifices?

In stark contrast, Holy Orders offer a different kind of martial consecration. Priests, the spiritual warriors of our age, don the armor of God to lead their flocks through the dark valleys of doubt and despair. Each ordination marks the creation of a guardian for the faith, a shepherd to guide us to greener pastures and stiller waters.

If the anointing of the sick has a somber tone, it's only to mask the profound joy and hope it brings. This sacrament serves as a paradoxical healing. It prepares us for the final earthly journey, not with dread or resignation, but with the hope of eternal life. It's a mystical meeting, where Christ, the Divine Physician, tends to both body and soul. There's no greater horror than facing this last battle alone, and there's no greater relief than the assurance that we don't have to.

Let's not forget the role of the laity in this divine play. Attending Mass and receiving the sacraments isn't a spectator sport. Active participation means more than just kneeling and standing at the right times. Bring your heart, bring your doubts, your fears, your everything. Let them be consumed and transformed by the sacred fire of divine love.

Yet, there's a cautionary tale here. Skipping Mass may start as an occasional slip but could morph into spiritual malnourishment. The soul, deprived of the spiritual succor provided by the sacraments, dwindles into a spectral existence. Imagine the horror of finding your spiritual self shriveled and weakened, a mere echo of the vibrant, God-breathed soul you were created to be.

The importance of Sunday Mass cannot be overstated. It's more than just an hour spent in prayer—it's a vital connection to the mystery of faith. It's here, amidst the prayers and the readings, that we recount the greatest love story ever told. The narrative arc of salvation history reaches a crescendo with the Eucharist. Here, the bread and wine become the body and blood of Christ, an unwavering testament to His infinite love and sacrifice.

In this sacred drama, the sacraments act as both plot points and life-saving interventions. Baptism sets us on the path, cleansing our original sin and marking our entry into the Christian community. The terrifying concept of being lost in the void of separation from God is banished with the cleansing waters of Baptism.

Confession offers an ongoing opportunity for renewal, a spiritual refresh button. But it's more than a mechanical reset. It's a deeply personal encounter with God's mercy, a confrontation with our own unworthiness, and a triumphant grasping of divine forgiveness. Sin is a horror that gnaws at the soul, but Confession douses this creeping terror with the balm of absolution.

The Eucharist, then, isn't just sustenance but a feast of love. Consider this: each time we receive Christ into our bodies, we become living tabernacles, thrones of the Almighty gracing the mundane walk of life. And there's humor in this paradox too—mirrors of divinity wandering through grocery store aisles and sitting in traffic jams!

The sacraments of Marriage and Holy Orders carry their unique brands of sanctity and struggle. Both require superhuman grace, a kind of spiritual iron-will that's as much a gift as it is a burden. Each has its share of comic and tragic moments, scenes worthy of Shakespearean dramas. Holy mirth and holy terror dance a bewildering

Role of Sacramentals

In the bustling corridors of everyday life, we often search for tangible reminders of the spiritual realm—a realm that goes largely unseen but is deeply felt. Here, sacraments serve as sanctifying, grace-bestowing pillars of our faith. But what of the objects that don't fit neatly into the Sacraments? Enter sacramentals, those blessed items that stand as physical reverberations of divine love and protection.

Sacramentals, while distinct from sacraments, hold a unique position in the spiritual lives of faithful Catholics. These items—such as holy water, rosaries, scapulars, medals, and ashes—are not just religious paraphernalia. They are deeply imbued with symbolism and possess the power to sanctify different aspects of our daily existence. Through them, the sacred seeps into the mundane, converting ordinary moments into opportunities for grace.

Imagine the humble crucifix hanging on a wall. To the uninitiated, it could simply be a piece of decor. But for the believer, it's a profound invocation of Christ's sacrifice. The crucifix doesn't just remind us of that fateful day at Golgotha; it challenges us to live with courage, self-sacrifice, and humility. It becomes a daily call to carry our own crosses, no matter their weight.

Let's not forget the role of holy water, an apparently simple mixture of salt and water that undergoes a sanctifying transformation through blessing. A sprinkle of holy water upon entering a church is a gesture loaded with significance. This act doesn't just refresh the body; it cleanses the spirit, recalling the purity of baptism. How many times have you gone home troubled, only to have a peaceful night of sleep after blessing yourself and your home with holy water? It's more than tradition; it's divine intervention through a few blessed drops.

The rosary is another powerful sacramental that holds more than just beads. As you move through its beads, each prayer becomes a rhythm, a heartbeat synchronizing your soul with the mysteries of Christ. The rosary encourages meditative prayer, taking you on a spiritual journey through the joys, sorrows, glories, and luminous moments of Christ's life and the Blessed Virgin Mary's role in salvation history. The repetition is calming—like a spiritual lullaby—and fosters a deeper connection with the divine.

Scapulars may seem like simple pieces of cloth, but they are potent symbols of commitment and protection. The Brown Scapular, for instance, is associated with the Carmelite Order and symbolizes the wearer's devotion to Mary and her intercessory power. It's a wearable declaration of faith, a pledge that whoever dies wearing it shall not suffer eternal fire, a promise rooted in the apparition of Our Lady of Mount Carmel to Saint Simon Stock. Imagine the comfort one feels knowing they have Mary's mantle of protection about them. It's both an armor and a reminder to live honorably.

Medals, such as the Miraculous Medal, offer another layer of divine protection and intercession. Originating from visions granted to Saint Catherine Labouré, the Miraculous Medal showcases the Virgin Mary and has been a divine tool for countless miracles and conversions. Wearing it is like keeping a piece of heaven close to your heart, a token that breathes grace, protection, and even miraculous intervention.

The Ash Wednesday rite, where ashes are blessed and placed on the foreheads of the faithful, may serve as one of the starkest reminders of our mortality and need for repentance. "Remember that you are dust, and to dust, you shall return." These words, spoken during the distribution of ashes, encapsulate the essence of human fragility and the eternal call to holiness. When the ashes are washed away, the spiritual mark they leave lingers, compelling a deeper introspection and transformation.

But sacramentals are not just personal; they are communal. Processions featuring statues, relics, and icons transform towns and cities into living, breathing testaments to faith. When communities carry a statue of their patron saint through their streets, it is a collective act of faith and devotion, merging the sacred with the secular, consecrating the very space they inhabit. These processions are not merely public displays; they are acts of sanctification, extensions of how sacramentals reach into every part of our lives.

It would be a mistake to overlook the role of exorcised salt. A bit of blessed salt can be sprinkled around the home, in soup, or even mixed into holy water, acting as a sacramental with potent protective properties. The exorcised salt isn't a mystical charm but is rooted in the ancient tradition of exorcizing places of demonic influence. For those who feel the heavy weight of unseen darkness, the sacramental power of exorcised salt brings comfort and divine security.

In a way, sacramentals bridge the gap between heaven and Earth. They are conduits through which divine power flows into our daily lives, enriching our routines and imbuing them with spiritual significance. So, while they might appear as small practices or tokens, their influence is vast, stealthily sanctifying our journey towards a fulfilling spiritual life.

Using these physical items as spiritual aids also aids in focusing our distracted minds. In a world increasingly noisy and chaotic, sacramentals offer a tangible anchor, something that evokes the sacred and the holy in an instant. It is nearly impossible to pick up a rosary and not feel a sense of calm, a mental shift towards prayer and contemplation. There's a comfort in holding something that has been blessed, tangibly touched by the divine.

Humorously enough, ask any Catholic and they'll tell you stories of skepticism quickly turned to belief through sacramentals. One could chuckle at tales of holy water burning the skin, or how an indignant atheist discovered that a Miraculous Medal was, indeed, more than just jewelry. Such anecdotes serve both as warnings and heartening reminders of the sacramentals' real, spiritual potency.

To view sacramentals as mere relics of older practices or quaint traditions is to miss their profound impact. They are markers of faith, evidence of a living tradition that sees the divine hand in the minutiae of life. They remind us that God's grace isn't confined to lofty church rituals but is instead woven into the very fabric of our daily existence. Like hidden gems scattered in a vast, modern desert, they keep us oriented towards the divine, each small item a point of light guiding us home.

Incorporate sacramentals into your life as both a declaration of faith and an invitation for God's grace to enter into every aspect of your existence. They are God's gentle whispers and, at times, forceful nudges, urging you to walk the straight and narrow path. Consider them as spiritual bulwarks, standing ready to shield you from the tempests of life. With sacramentals, the battle for a fulfilling spiritual life isn't fought alone; it's a daily engagement enriched by divine grace.

Chapter 8: Love and Charity in Action

Continuing from our exploration of a fulfilling spiritual life, we now delve into the heart's expression through love and charity. Our faith calls us to act not just in words but in deeds, reflecting the divine love bestowed upon us. The saints, luminous beacons of selflessness, offer glorious examples of how to live this love daily. St. Vincent de Paul, with his unyielding commitment to the destitute, and Mother Teresa, whose hands were ever ready to comfort the unloved and the unseen, illuminate the path. Yet, the tradition of Catholic charity didn't halt with the saints; it finds vibrant expression today in countless acts of kindness that quietly transform lives. This chapter isn't merely a recounting of heroic deeds but an invitation to join this lineage of compassion, to let your love speak volumes, roar into action, and make the world a sanctuary of grace.

Acts of Love by Saints

Throughout history, saints have become beacons of divine love and charity, illuminating the path of righteousness through their selfless acts. Take St. Vincent de Paul, whose tireless efforts to aid the poor and sick are nothing short of legendary, or Mother Teresa, whose boundless compassion for the most destitute in Calcutta still inspires millions. These saints didn't just preach love; they lived it, in actions that spoke louder than words ever could. The sacrifices they made, often risking their lives and facing tremendous adversity, serve as a daunting reminder and a fierce motivator. Their stories, painted in vibrant hues of grace, remind us that our small acts of kindness carry the weight of divine love, capable of transforming hearts and lives. By emulating these acts of love, we too can aspire to be instruments of God's grace, spreading hope, compassion, and charity in a world sorely in need of all three.

St. Vincent de Paul's Charity is a beacon of Christian virtue, illuminating the path with love that is both profound and practical. St. Vincent, known as the "Father of the Poor," showed us that true charity transcends mere philanthropy. It is not just about giving, but about living the Gospel through selfless service, turning compassion into action.

Born in 1581 in the small French village of Pouy, Vincent was ordained a priest at the tender age of nineteen. His early days were marred by ambitions of climbing the ecclesiastical ranks, but God had a transformative plan for him. Captured by Turkish pirates and sold into slavery in Tunis, Vincent's heart found a new direction in the very crucible of suffering. His eventual escape was nothing short of miraculous, and it marked the beginning of a life devoted to alleviating the burdens of others.

Vincent's charity work was revolutionary not just for its scope, but for its method. He founded the Congregation of the Mission, commonly known as the Vincentians, who dedicated themselves to preaching and pastoral care, particularly in rural areas often neglected by the Church. He also established the Daughters of Charity with St. Louise de Marillac, an order that broke the mold by working outside cloisters, serving the poor directly in their homes and hovels, hospitals, and orphanages.

One vivid episode of Vincent's charity that still haunts the halls of history involved the galley slaves of Paris. Chained and condemned to rowing without end, these men were little more than living corpses. When Vincent encountered them, his heart shattered at their plight. Not content with only providing spiritual comfort, he advocated tirelessly for their humane treatment and better living conditions, creating hospitals and shelters specifically for their welfare. In doing so, he was a voice where there was none, a flicker of divine mercy in a dark world.

The intriguing paradoxes of St. Vincent's life paint a larger-than-life figure who was at once unassuming but deeply impactful. He was both compassionate and fiercely practical, a man who understood that miracles often follow hard work and organization. Not one to shy away from the nitty-gritty, he knew that lofty ideals had to be grounded in actionable plans to bear fruit. Through soup kitchens, hostels for the homeless, and enduring community support systems, he left a legacy that extends far beyond his earthly life.

St. Vincent's spiritual philosophy also carried a stern warning. He recognized the inherent dignity in every soul and the responsibility of the faithful to uphold it. His horror at social injustices was not passive. He understood that neglecting the poor was tantamount to neglecting Christ himself—a frightful realization that was meant to spur the complacent into action. His very life was a testament to Matthew 25:40: "Whatever you did for one of the least of these brothers and sisters of mine, you did for me."

In today's context, St. Vincent's model of charity is as critical as ever. The face of modern poverty may have shifted, but the underlying issues remain. Homelessness, hunger, and despair are rampant. It's easy to be paralyzed by the enormity of these problems, but Vincent teaches us that the solution lies in collective, unwavering efforts. Each act of kindness, no matter how small, can reverberate through society, creating ripples of change. Imagine the world if we all adopted even a fraction of his zeal and compassion.

One compelling instance showcases his profound impact. During a devastating famine that swept through Paris in the early 17th century, Vincent leveraged his network to orchestrate an almost Herculean relief effort. He mobilized resources from wealthy benefactors and coordinated massive food distributions, ensuring those hardest hit received sustenance and hope. This was charity in its truest form—sustained, organized, and driven by a relentless love for humanity. It's an exhibition of faith wielded like a sword against the encroaching darkness of despair.

And let's not forget the importance of humor—a tool Vincent used astutely to navigate the often somber world of charity. He believed that laughter and joy were integral to the human spirit. Stories from his life are peppered with moments when his wit helped demystify complex theological principles or diffuse tense situations. His humor wasn't frivolous, but a means of connecting with people on an emotional level, making his Gospel message that much more accessible and impactful.

Vincent de Paul's life was also a vivid tapestry of motivational and inspirational threads woven together. When cynics and skeptics questioned the sustainability of his charitable works, he replied with feats that silenced criticism and inspired awe. He showed that faith could move mountains—both literal and metaphorical. His very existence demands that we, too, embrace the transformative power of charity, challenging ourselves to see Christ in every face we encounter.

Engaging with modern Catholic charitable organizations, one can see Vincent's enduring influence. Institutions like the Society of St. Vincent de Paul continue his mission globally, providing programs for housing, job training, disaster relief, and more. This legacy isn't confined within church walls but extends into the very fabric of secular society, proving that true charity transcends barriers and impacts lives profoundly.

Vincent de Paul didn't just feed the hungry or clothe the naked; he resurrected hope where it had died, kindled faith where it had waned, and lit the path for countless others to follow. His message, steeped in dedication and cloaked in sincere humility, whispers through the ages: "To serve is to save."

To close on an inspirational note, reimagine the very essence of Vincent's work—love in action. It's easy to get overwhelmed by the magnitude of need that exists, but Vincent's life simplifies it into actionable steps. His charity wasn't limited by grand gestures but was realized through consistent, everyday acts of love. This is the legacy we are

called to continue: to look beyond ourselves,
to see Christ in our neighbor, and to
believe, unwaveringly, in the boundless power
of divinely inspired charity.

Mother Teresa's Missionary Work is one of the most profound examples of love and charity in action, a living testament to the power of faith combined with relentless compassion. Mother Teresa, born Agnes Gonxha Bojaxhiu in 1910, became synonymous with selfless service to the poorest of the poor. She founded the Missionaries of Charity in 1950, an order that would grow to have thousands of members and serve in over 100 countries.

Now, imagine a frail, elderly woman, draped in a simple white sari edged with blue, navigating through the bustling, chaotic streets of Calcutta. Among the overwhelming noise and sights, she saw something beyond the human eye—a divine mission. The streets, littered with the destitute and diseased, became her sanctuary. With a heart brimming with love for Christ, Mother Teresa took up the cross of the oppressed and downtrodden.

A picture of serenity in the eye of the storm, her work began in the slums, where human pain was raw and unfiltered. She established Nirmal Hriday, which translates to "Pure Heart," a hospice where the dying were given the dignity of a loving touch in their final moments. This was not just charity; it was a profound act of witnessing the face of Christ in the suffering.

Yet, humor was never far from her lips. She often quipped that she was just "a little pencil in the hands of God." Her simplicity and boundless love drew people from all walks of life into her mission. Volunteers flocked to her side, not because of grand speeches or fervent pleas, but due to the magnetic pull of genuine, Christ-like love.

Mother Teresa's mission wasn't just about alleviating physical hunger, though that was a significant part. She aimed to feed the spiritual starvation that plagued many. "One of the greatest diseases," she noted, "is to be nobody to anybody." These words carried an echo of horror, reflecting a world losing its heart. In stark contrast, her actions inspired humor-filled reflections on how the smallest deeds can mend the fabric of society.

Despite the monstrous scale of poverty she faced, Mother Teresa never succumbed to despair. Instead, she motivated others to see that even the darkest glimmers of life were fragments of God's plan. She encouraged people to perform acts of kindness—each one, a stitch in the tattered quilt of humanity. "Not all of us can do great things," she famously said, "but we can do small things with great love."

Mother Teresa's Missionary Work often read like chapters from a spiritual thriller. Disturbing scenes of disease and neglect were transformed through acts of mercy and grace. Children abandoned on street corners found sanctuary in orphanages she established. Those battling leprosy discovered community and acceptance, shattering the horror of isolation.

Her work, while deeply spiritual, wasn't devoid of practical wisdom. She recognized that systemic change was essential and worked tirelessly to improve healthcare, education, and social services. In collaboration with governments and other organizations, Mother

Teresa helped set up schools, mobile health clinics, and nutrition programs. Her spiritual drive was complemented by a pragmatic approach that addressed both the symptom and the disease.

There were times when her humor shone through her tireless labor. When asked how she managed to keep going, she would respond with a twinkle in her eye, "I am God's pencil. He does all the writing; I just try to stay out of his way." Her wit was a balm, a subtle reminder that joy and faith need not be divorced from duty.

Each day, she encountered new horrors—children suffering from malnutrition, families torn apart by disease, and elderly people discarded by society. But for every soul saved, there was a spark of hope, a miracle that defied the gloom. Stories of conversions were not uncommon. People drawn to her mission often found themselves transformed, their lives redirected towards paths of righteousness.

Mother Teresa's Missionary Work was sustained by an unyielding faith, a belief that she was called to be a servant of Christ in the least of his brethren. Despite personal struggles, including periods of spiritual darkness, she pressed on. Her letters reveal an inner torment, a seeming contradiction to her outward joy. But this only humanized her, making her all the more relatable to those wrestling with their own faith.

Perhaps the most striking aspect of her work was the sense of inclusivity. Mother Teresa never distinguished between creed, caste, or color. Her love was as universal as the gospel she preached. Muslims, Hindus, Christians—all were recipients of her boundless charity. She embodied the parable of the Good Samaritan, crossing religious and social boundaries to offer mercy.

Mother Teresa wasn't just a saint in a distant, hagiographic sense. She was a woman who trod the same earth as us, faced the same darkness, yet illuminated the world with a divine light. Her work is a clarion call to engage more deeply with our faith, to transform our beliefs into actions that heal and uplift. She showed that love and humor, coupled with faith, could indeed perform miracles.

In essence, **Mother Teresa's Missionary Work** is an epic saga of divine love beating against the currents of despair. It is a reminder that faith isn't an abstract concept, but a living, breathing force capable of altering the course of history. As Catholics and seekers of truth, we are invited to not just admire her legacy but to take up our own small crosses and walk in her footsteps, showing that love is the most potent weapon against the darkness of our times.

Modern Examples of Catholic Charity

Catholic charity is a radiant, enduring beacon, providing light and hope in a world perpetually grappling with darkness. This light manifests in numerous ways across the modern landscape, illuminating paths for the weary and bringing solace to the distressed. Let us delve into contemporary examples of this profound virtue that continue to resonate with and inspire the faithful.

Consider the humbling work of Catholic Relief Services (CRS). Founded by the United States Conference of Catholic Bishops, CRS embodies the Church's warm embrace, extending its reach to over 100 countries. They tackle a spectrum of global crises, from emergency responses in the aftermath of natural disasters to long-term developmental projects in impoverished communities. When a devastating earthquake struck Haiti in 2010, CRS was on the ground within hours, providing food, shelter, and medical care to thousands. It's a testament to the Church's unwavering commitment to transforming lives through love and compassion.

Another cornerstone of modern Catholic charity is the St. Vincent de Paul Society, which operates tirelessly around the world. This organization, founded by Blessed Frédéric Ozanam in 1833, focuses on person-to-person assistance. The society's volunteers, often called "Vincentians," engage in a myriad of charitable acts—from visiting the sick and elderly to providing financial assistance and advocating for social justice. Picture a Vincentian quietly knocking on the door of a struggling family, armed with nothing but groceries and a heart full of empathy. It's these intimate, often unseen gestures that breathe life into the Gospel's command to love one's neighbor.

On a more localized scale, many dioceses and parishes have initiated creative programs that cater to specific community needs. Take, for example, the "Lazarus House" in St. Louis, Missouri—a sanctuary for homeless individuals run by a group of dedicated parishioners. Here, the homeless find not just a hot meal and a place to sleep, but a sense of dignity and belonging. Such initiatives show that charity is not merely about alleviating physical suffering; it's also about restoring human dignity.

In the digital age, even online platforms have become vessels for Catholic charity. Websites like "Missio," launched by the Pontifical Mission Societies, allow users to support various mission projects across the globe. With just a few clicks, a donor can contribute to building a school in Uganda or providing clean water to a village in Bolivia. This technological bridge reaffirms that the heart of charity beats stronger than ever, adapting to modern means to reach those in need.

Of course, no discussion of modern Catholic charity would be complete without mentioning the influential role of Catholic healthcare systems. Hospitals and clinics run by Catholic organizations are often at the forefront of providing compassionate care, especially to the underserved. During the COVID-19 pandemic, Catholic hospitals were critical in their communities, offering not just medical treatment but spiritual comfort as well. These institutions don't just heal bodies; they minister to souls, offering a holistic approach to health rooted in the sanctity of human life.

Educational initiatives also play a key role in contemporary Catholic charity. Programs like the Cristo Rey Network provide quality education to students from low-income families, equipping them with the skills necessary for success in both college and the workforce. The network's innovative model, which includes corporate work-study opportunities, helps break the chains of poverty through education, a truly transformative act of charity.

Missionaries of Charity, founded by St. Teresa of Calcutta, continue their incredible work today. Operating in multiple countries, these sisters, brothers, and laypeople echo Mother Teresa's mission to care for "the poorest of the poor." They run hospices, orphanages, and schools, providing not just material aid but also the priceless gift of love. The enduring legacy of Mother Teresa's work is a vivid reminder that true charity transcends time and place, rooted deeply in the love of Christ.

Modern Catholic charity also extends to advocacy and justice work. Organizations like the Catholic Campaign for Human Development (CCHD) focus on addressing the root causes of poverty and injustice. Through grants and community-based projects, CCHD supports innovative initiatives that empower marginalized communities. This proactive approach ensures that charity is not just about temporary relief but about fostering long-term change and equity.

In today's interconnected world, modern Catholic charity is also characterized by interfaith cooperation. By collaborating with other religious groups, Catholics demonstrate that the essence of charity transcends doctrinal boundaries. Initiatives like "The Abraham Accords" feature collaboration between Catholic, Jewish, and Muslim organizations, all working together to promote peace and humanitarian aid globally. Such efforts underscore the Catholic Church's commitment to unity and the universal call to love one's neighbor.

The social media age, often criticized for fostering superficial connections, also offers unprecedented platforms for spreading charitable initiatives. Catholic influencers and organizations harness these tools to mobilize resources and raise awareness about various causes. Campaigns like "40 Days for Life," a community-based pro-life campaign, effectively use social media to organize prayer vigils and halt abortions—an embodiment of charity in modern activism.

While institutional efforts are substantial, individual acts of charity also shine brightly in today's Catholic landscape. Stories abound of everyday Catholics who, inspired by their faith, make profound impacts through simple acts of kindness. A single mother who fosters children, a businessman who anonymously pays off medical debts, or a teenager who organizes a food drive—all these examples reflect the enduring spirit of Catholic charity.

Even amidst contemporary challenges, from economic disparities to ecological crises, the tenets of Catholic charity provide a guiding light. Pope Francis, through his encyclicals like "Laudato Si'," calls for a renewed commitment to environmental stewardship, seeing it as a form of charity to future generations. By advocating for sustainable practices and care for creation, Catholics today extend their charity beyond human beings to embrace the entire planet.

To encapsulate the myriad forms of modern Catholic charity would be akin to bottling the ocean. However, the essence remains the same: a dynamic, living testament to Christ's love, an unwavering commitment to serve and uplift the less fortunate. Each charitable act, whether grand or humble, contributes to a broader tapestry of grace and compassion, furthering the Kingdom of God on earth.

As we look upon these modern examples, we're reminded that charity is not confined to grand gestures; it is woven into the fabric of everyday life, manifesting in myriad forms and reaching into the deepest recesses of human suffering. It is our call, our mission, to embody this purest form of love, ensuring that the light of charity never dims but continues to guide us and those we serve toward eternal salvation.

Chapter 9: The Joy of Hope

Amidst the labyrinthine corridors of life's trials, the joy of hope shines like a divine beacon, guiding souls through the enveloping darkness. Think of St. Monica, whose relentless prayers and hopes for her wayward son, Augustine, were eventually rewarded with his conversion and sainthood. How magnificent it is to witness hope fulfilled! Consider also St. Jude, revered as the patron saint of desperate cases, who turned countless hearts from despair to faith through miraculous interventions. Hope is not a fleeting sentiment but a steadfast anchor that holds even when stormy waves threaten to capsize our spirits. Through laughter and tears, triumphs and tribulations, hope transforms every shadowed corner into a sanctuary of light, reminding us that, though the night is dark, the promise of dawn remains unwavering and eternal. Let the stories of these saints be a lantern, illuminating your path and igniting a fire within to persevere, no matter the adversity.

Stories of Hope Fulfilled

Within the tapestry of human experience, few threads shine brighter than the stories where hope is not just a distant dream but a reality touched by divine grace. Consider St. Monica, whose relentless prayers and unyielding faith brought about the conversion of her wayward son, St. Augustine. Then there is the story of St. Jude, the patron saint of lost causes, whose intersessions have led to miraculous outcomes in seemingly hopeless situations. These narratives, drenched in a potent mixture of fervent prayer and divine intervention, serve to inspire and uplift. They challenge us to cling to hope amidst adversity, reminding us that with faith, all things are possible. These tales illuminate the path for those seeking the truth, urging us all to remain steadfast and filled with hope, no matter the darkness surrounding us.

St. Monica and St. Augustine unearthed one of the most profound testaments of a mother's love and the power of spiritual transformation. Their lives, filled with fervor, agony, and miracles, brilliantly illuminate the divine symphony of faith and redemption, striking chords of hope and perseverance in our hearts.

Born in Tagaste, a small town in North Africa, Monica was a devout Christian married to Patricius, a pagan with a volatile disposition. Despite his fiery temper and infidelity, Monica's unwavering faith and kindness eventually led to Patricius's conversion to Christianity. However, her greatest challenge was yet to come: converting her wayward son, Augustine.

The story of St. Augustine's early life is anything but saintly. A brilliant but rebellious young man, Augustine indulged in worldly pleasures and clung to heretical beliefs. Much to Monica's despair, he left home to pursue studies in Carthage, where he further strayed from Christian teachings. Her once-dutiful son became enraptured by the

Manichean religion, a belief system that starkly opposed the Christ-centered faith Monica cherished.

Monica, however, was not to be dissuaded. With a heart full of anger, anguish, and love, she followed Augustine to Carthage and then to Rome, and finally to Milan. Her unyielding prayers and rivers of tears encapsulated the essence of a mother's relentless hope. Day and night, Monica pleaded with God for her son's conversion, epitomizing the Biblical adage: "Pray without ceasing".

Now, let's dwell on the famous episode where Monica's earnest weeping moved Ambrose, the Bishop of Milan. Ambrose consoled her with words that have since echoed through centuries: "It is not possible that the son of so many tears should perish." With truth wrapped in loving encouragement, Ambrose's prophecy would soon unfold in an extraordinary manner.

Augustine's encounter with St. Ambrose proved pivotal. Though initially seeking to hone his oratory skills by listening to Ambrose's sermons, Augustine found himself irresistibly drawn to the bishop's teachings. His heart, once hardened with skepticism and pride, began to soften. Monica's relentless prayers, combined with Ambrose's intellectual and spiritual influence, initiated a seismic shift within Augustine.

During this period of turmoil and transformation, Augustine penned his spiritual autobiography, "Confessions". This literary masterpiece offers a lucid window into his struggle with faith, morality, and his ultimate surrender to God's grace. Augustine recounts a poignant moment in a garden where he heard a child's voice chanting, "Take up and read". Interpreting this as a divine command, he opened the Scriptures and read a passage from St. Paul's Letter to the Romans, which urged him to abandon sinful desires and "put on the Lord Jesus Christ."

The grand metamorphosis culminated in Augustine receiving baptism from St. Ambrose at the Easter Vigil in 387. The event marked the zenith of Monica's prayers. Her tears had been transformed into tears of joy, witnessing her son's embrace of the faith she held so dearly. Indeed, her dogged perseverance had borne the sweetest fruit.

The saga of St. Monica and St. Augustine doesn't end with mere conversion. Augustine's life thereafter exemplified a burning zeal for God. Ordained a priest and later a bishop, he became one of the most influential Church Fathers. His theological insights and prolific writings have had an enduring impact on Christian thought, deeply enriching the doctrine of grace, free will, and the nature of the Church.

One can almost marvel at the divine choreography that orchestrated their lives. God's providence moved through Monica's maternal tenacity and Augustine's intellectual quest, weaving a tale that continues to offer hope to families worldwide. Parents praying for their wayward children find solace in Monica's steadfast example, while sinners battling their inner demons can look to Augustine's conversion as a beacon of hope.

The emotional depth of Monica and Augustine's story mirrors the trials faced by many today. It isn't just a narrative of ancient saints; it's an ongoing testament to the transformative power of faith and prayer, rendering the impossible possible. Monica's life amplifies the belief that no soul is beyond God's reach, and Augustine resonates this by exemplifying how intellectual rigor and spiritual humility can coexist to create a profound spiritual legacy.

In contemplating the unbreakable bond between Monica and Augustine, we find ourselves inspired to cultivate unyielding hope. Amidst tears and trials, faith can still carve out a path to redemption. Monica and Augustine teach us that fervent prayers, unwavering hope, and ceaseless love can indeed manifest miracles, not only for ourselves but for those we hold dear.

The legacy of St. Monica and St. Augustine challenges us to be relentless in our faith and unyielding in our prayers. They whisper to us in our darkest moments, urging us to believe, to hope, and never to give up. For in the grand tapestry of God's plan, even our deepest sorrows and our most wayward moments can be woven into threads of divine love and grace. Their lives, filled with struggle and eventual triumph, shine a light on the infinite possibilities of God's mercy, making their story an eternal source of inspiration for us all.

St. Jude and His Devotion holds a special place in the hearts of many Catholics as the patron saint of lost causes and desperate situations. His devotion is a testament to a life of unwavering faith, a life that continues to inspire and uplift countless believers in their darkest moments. St. Jude, one of the twelve apostles of Jesus, often occupies a unique position in the communion of saints, representing hope and courage in the face of seemingly insurmountable odds.

Imagine being tasked with a mission that seems utterly impossible. St. Jude's life was fraught with challenges that could easily have led him to despair. Yet, this humble apostle chose to transform obstacles into opportunities for divine intervention. Known as Jude Thaddeus, he was relentless in spreading the teachings of Christ across Pagan lands, undeterred by the specter of persecution and rejection.

One cannot discuss St. Jude's devotion without mentioning the epistle that bears his name. This brief but potent letter, found in the New Testament, is an exhortation to the early Christians to contend for their faith. With fervor and urgency, St. Jude warns against false teachings and moral degradation, urging believers to remain steadfast in love and prayer. He envisioned a community that mirrored Christ's own commitment to truth and justice, a vision that continues to resonate in modern times. Let's delve deeper into St. Jude's inspiring devotion and its various facets.

St. Jude's intercessory power is another aspect of his devotion that merits attention. Over the centuries, countless miracles have been attributed to his prayers. These aren't merely anecdotes from a distant past; they are the lived experiences of individuals whose lives were radically transformed through his intervention. Take, for instance, the story of a woman on the brink of financial ruin, who turned to St. Jude in her desperation. Within days, she received unexpected funds that allowed her to avoid bankruptcy and rebuild her life. Instances like these aren't isolated; they are the norm in St. Jude's long history of miracles.

For a saint often depicted with a flame over his head—symbolizing the Holy Spirit—St. Jude's devotion is indeed fervent. He's often shown with an image of Christ, underscoring his close relationship with the Savior. This visual symbolism serves as a powerful reminder that, even in desperate circumstances, the light of Christ can guide us through the darkest of times. It's a beacon of hope that St. Jude carries for all who seek his intercession.

It's not just the grand miracles that define St. Jude's devotion. Often, it's the quiet, subtle interventions that reveal the depth of his faith. Tales of families reconciled, illnesses healed, and spirits uplifted through his prayers paint a comprehensive picture of a saint deeply committed to alleviating human suffering. St. Jude teaches us that no prayer is too small, no problem too insignificant for divine attention.

In art and literature, St. Jude is frequently portrayed with a club or an axe, symbolizing his martyrdom. Tradition holds that he was martyred for his unwavering commitment to

Christ. This ultimate sacrifice is perhaps the greatest testament to his devotion. He didn't merely preach faith; he lived and died for it, embodying the very essence of spiritual perseverance. His martyrdom serves as a stark, if horrifying, reminder of the cost of true devotion and the incredible strength required to sustain it.

St. Jude's influence extends beyond the individual to entire communities. Many churches and institutions, particularly those focused on healthcare and social services, bear his name. They strive to mirror his devotion by serving those in despair and offering hope where it's needed most. St. Jude Children's Research Hospital, for instance, stands as a monumental testament to his enduring legacy, providing free care to children with catastrophic diseases. This kind of institution embodies the practical application of his teachings, forming a bridge between faith and action.

We mustn't overlook the personal element of St. Jude's devotion. For many, turning to St. Jude is akin to calling an old friend who understands their plight. His followers often recount feeling an inexplicable peace after praying for his intercession, a sense of being heard and understood. This deeply personal connection transforms their faith from a series of rituals into a living, breathing relationship with the divine.

Let's address the humor that pervades St. Jude's narrative. It's not the laughter of frivolity but the profound joy that springs from faith overcoming adversity. St. Jude himself, in his unwavering devotion, might have chuckled at the irony of being known as the patron of hopeless causes. After all, his life was anything but hopeless. It's a testament to the divine comedy, the surprising ways in which God's grace manifests in our lives.

In the grand tapestry of Catholic saints, St. Jude's devotion stands as a vibrant thread, a source of hope and inspiration. His life, miracles, and martyrdom encapsulate the essence of unwavering faith and divine intervention. As we navigate our own challenges, St. Jude encourages us to persist, to seek the divine in our despair, and to trust that, even in our darkest hours, the light of Christ will guide us. Through his intercession, we find the strength to face the impossible, the courage to persevere, and the inspiration to live out our faith with the same fervor that defined his extraordinary life.

So, as you ponder the legacy of St. Jude and his devotion, remember that this isn't just an ancient tale but a living testament to the power of faith. It's a call to action, a reminder that through perseverance and trust in divine providence, no situation is truly hopeless. St. Jude continues to be a guiding light for those in need, a beacon of hope that encourages us to face life's challenges with courage and conviction. His life exemplifies the transformative power of unwavering faith and inspires us to carry the torch forward, illuminating the path for others.

Maintaining Hope Amidst Adversity

Amidst life's storms, hope stands as an unyielding beacon, drawing strength from faith and a resolute spirit. Whether it's a sudden illness, financial strain, or a crisis of faith, each form of adversity serves as a crucible for hope. The life of a Roman Catholic, much like any other faithful soul, weaves through moments of darkness and light. But within the Catholic tradition lies a rich tapestry of guidance and inspiration, urging believers to clutch hope tightly, even when the night seems interminable.

Consider the trials of Job, that quintessential figure of steadfastness in the Bible. His unwavering belief, despite monumental losses and suffering, paints a vivid picture for us. Job's hope wasn't a naive optimism but a deep-seated trust in God's ultimate wisdom and justice. His story reminds us that hope doesn't mean denying harsh realities but rather facing them with a firm belief in divine providence.

Our own lives may not be recorded in holy script, nor might our tribulations be as cataclysmic, but the principle remains unchanged. Hope amidst adversity requires the resilience of a battle-hardened soldier and the simplicity of a child's trust. When life's waves crash violently upon the shores of our existence, hope acts as the lighthouse guiding us safely to harbor.

Take, for instance, the story of St. Monica. Here was a woman who faced the profound sorrow of seeing her son, Augustine, stray far from the path of righteousness. Yet, through years of fervent prayer and unwavering hope, she became a living testament to the power of hopeful persistence. Her story serves as a reminder that sometimes, the wait for divine intervention can stretch over years, testing the very limits of our patience and faith.

Adversity often arrives uninvited, bringing with it the echo of despair. It's easy to feel abandoned, as if the heavens have rolled shut, keeping their solace and answers hidden. But it's precisely in these moments that the teachings of the Church encourage us to double down on our hope. The words of St. Paul in his letter to the Romans come to mind: "Rejoice in hope, be patient in tribulation, be constant in prayer" (Romans 12:12). This triad of rejoicing, patience, and prayer forms the bedrock upon which an unshakeable hope is built.

There's a peculiar humor in the human condition, a divine irony, if you will. Just when we think our strength is exhausted, a flicker of hope often emerges from the most unexpected quarters. Sometimes, it's a fleeting moment of peace in prayer, other times a kind word from a friend or a seemingly coincidental blessing that reignites the flame within us. Divine providence, it seems, loves to work in mysterious ways.

Even saints who faced unimaginable adversities found a way to sustain hope. St. Maximilian Kolbe, confined within the cold, brutal walls of Auschwitz, offered himself in place of another prisoner. In an environment designed to crush the human spirit, he became a beacon of hope. His ultimate sacrifice was not just an act of love but a rebellion against despair itself, telling us in no uncertain terms that hope can reside even in the darkness of a death camp.

Hope isn't a monolithic experience; it's a mosaic of countless small acts and thoughts. When St. Therese of Lisieux spoke of her "little way," she was emphasizing the power of small deeds done with great love. Our daily struggles might seem insignificant on the grand scale of holy wars and saintly sacrifices, but they are no less vital. Each act of kindness, each whispered prayer, fortifies our hope and shapes our journey.

Contemporary life has its own breed of tribulations. The constant barrage of information, the pressures of modern living, and the pervasiveness of secularism can make holding onto hope a Herculean task. Yet, the Church provides timeless wisdom to anchor us. Practices such as attending Mass, regular confession, and the use of sacramentals are not mere rituals but lifelines. They tether us to a spiritual reality that transcends the vicissitudes of daily life.

In times of adversity, humor often becomes an unexpected ally. Stories and jokes from the lives of saints and popes show us that even in the gravest circumstances, a light-hearted spirit can be a potent antidote to despair. Humor doesn't trivialize our trials; instead, it gives us the strength to face them with a smile, finding joy in the absurdities and unexpected turns of life.

St. Philip Neri, known for his humorous approach to holiness, once remarked, "A joyful heart is more easily made perfect than a downcast one." His words ring true, reminding us that the power of laughter and joy shouldn't be underestimated. These moments of levity serve as necessary counterpoints to the weight of our struggles, allowing us to navigate adversity without losing our hope.

Then there's the matter of communal support. Adversity can often feel like a solitary journey, but the Church community offers a shelter of solidarity. It's in the shared prayers and collective strength of the faithful that hope finds a fertile ground to grow. The rosary circles, prayer meetings, and fellowship gatherings act like pockets of respite, refueling our hope when it wanes.

The teachings and lives of saints also serve as a divine roadmap. When faced with adversity, we can turn to the stories of those who have trodden similar paths before us. The lives of lesser-known saints, like St. Josephine Bakhita and St. Andre Bessette, offer rich narratives of hope persevering against all odds. Their stories might lack the grandeur of more famous saintly sagas, but they possess an accessibility and relatability that render them powerful guides in our own journeys.

It's easy to romanticize the concept of hope, but it is, in essence, a gritty, determined endeavor. It's not just about the lofty aspirations of eternal salvation but about finding the strength to face each new day despite the shadows that loom. The transformative power of hope lies not in grand gestures but in the quiet resolve to hold on, one day at a time.

Let's not forget the transformative power of repentance as well. In turning away from sin and back towards God, we find new wells of hope opening up. Stories like that of St. Mary Magdalene, redeemed through her profound contrition, highlight that hope isn't just a passive expectation of better times but an active turning towards the light. In repentance, we constantly renew our commitment to hope.

Ultimately, maintaining hope amidst adversity is about continuing the journey with trust and perseverance. It's about believing that, no matter how rough the path may be, there is a greater purpose and a divine plan that we might not yet comprehend. Hope transforms our perception of adversity, not by sweeping it away but by illuminating the divine grace that sustains us through it.

As we navigate this labyrinth of trials, let us remember that our faith arms us with the hope needed to emerge victorious. Every challenge faced with hope

Chapter 10: Lessons from Purgatory and Hell

As we traverse through the mysterious realms of Purgatory and Hell, the lessons bestowed upon us are both harrowing and enlightening. Imagine, if you will, souls in a state of purgation, enduring the cleansing fires with hope burning brighter than the flames themselves. Their sufferings whisper to us the importance of repentance, the value of every sacrament, and the gravity of each sin committed on earth. Then, we turn our gaze to Hell—a place not of folklore, but of stark, terrifying reality that saints like St. Faustina and Padre Pio have vividly recounted. The torments there, void of hope, echo the dire need to turn away from sin while time permits. Through the frightful visions and fervent teachings of these holy figures, we comprehend the immense love and justice of God. These stark revelations become our guideposts, urging us to embrace the path of righteousness with renewed fervor, lest we too face such torment. And so, let this profound duality of Purgatory's hope and Hell's despair drive us forward with a resolute heart, ever mindful of our eternal destiny.

Saints' Warnings and Teachings

As if the pages of history were alive, saints from every age have urgently called out to us about the perils of sin and the eternal consequences that lurk in both Purgatory and Hell. Their visions and accounts don't just paint a picture; they etch a vivid horror and urgency into our very souls. Saint Faustina, with her haunting visions, and Padre Pio, with his piercing insights, didn't mince words as they beckoned sinners to repentance, often with an alarming gravity that shakes us to our core. These revered figures, blessed with divine revelations, serve as both harbingers of caution and luminous beacons leading us toward the path of righteousness. They're not here to merely frighten us but to instill a reverential fear of God, one that propels us toward transformation and salvation. Saints' admonitions are not relics of the past but rather eternal echoes urging us to steer clear of damnation and embrace the redemption offered by God's infinite mercy.

St. Faustina's Visions did not merely offer glimpses into the ethereal but presented profound revelations, weaving together threads of mercy, judgment, and repentance. Saint Faustina Kowalska, known as the Apostle of Divine Mercy, had her life deeply intertwined with the mystical. Her visions, chronicled meticulously in her "Diary: Divine Mercy in My Soul," describe her spiritual encounters with Jesus and experiences of Purgatory and Hell. These were not whimsical flights of fancy but intense spiritual exercises that bore fruit in her unyielding message of divine mercy.

Through St. Faustina's eyes, one could see the spiritual warfare raging beyond the veil of mortal existence. Her visions were a mix of serene encounters with the divine and harrowing glimpses of the afterlife's torments. She often narrated how she was taken to the realms of purgation and eternal damnation, seeing souls in agony and hearing their heart-wrenching cries. Lest you think this is the stuff of fairy tales, her accounts were visceral and rooted in her unshakeable faith.

One vision that stands out, recorded on October 5, 1936, is particularly chilling. St. Faustina described how Jesus took her to the bottomless depths of Hell. She observed various torments suffered by the damned souls and noted distinct forms of punishment. The way she depicted the suffering was profoundly affective and descriptive: endless fire, lamentation, and the gnashing of teeth. Yet it wasn't just the fiery torment that gave pause but the eternal separation from God. A sort of emptiness that gnawed at the very essence of the soul.

These terrifying glimpses, however, were not visions given for the sake of horror. St. Faustina was repeatedly shown these scenes to underscore the urgency of repentance and God's unfathomable mercy. In her diary, Jesus reiterates the offer of mercy to even the gravest of sinners. One does not need to be a saint overnight, but one must recognize one's faults, seek repentance, and revel in divine mercy. For Faustina, these visions were both an invitation and a warning.

In contrast to the horror-filled scenery of Hell, St. Faustina's experiences of Purgatory were imbued with a sense of purification and hope. She describes souls who endure temporary suffering to be purified of their sins, awaiting the time they are worthy to join the divine presence in Heaven. Despite the purgative pains, these visions carried a sense of eventual reunion with God, serving as a profound reminder of the need for intercessory prayers from the living. St. Faustina's unwavering commitment to praying for these souls highlights a core tenet of Catholic teaching: the communion of saints and the power of prayer.

For those seeking inspiration, her encounters with Jesus provide a striking contrast to her harrowing visions of Hell. Rather than depicting Him merely as a stern judge, St. Faustina's visions frequently emphasize His infinite mercy. On one occasion, she saw the rays of mercy flowing from His heart, a vivid theophany that she famously depicted in the

Divine Mercy image. Jesus urged her to promote this devotion, promising that souls who venerated it would receive abundant graces.

It's hard to imagine the emotional and psychological weight such visions would impart on anyone, let alone a humble nun living in pre-war Poland. Faustina, however, bore this burden gracefully. Her life stands as testimony to the power of embracing both divine beauty and existential horror, thus leading a path for the faithful to tread with eyes wide open, seeing both the light and the dark.

Yet, it's important to remember the context in which these visions occurred. In the 1930s, the world was teetering on the brink of immense turmoil, and Poland itself was soon to become engulfed in the horrors of World War II. In such a context, Faustina's messages of mercy and the terrifying reality of rejecting it became all the more poignant. They came not just as personal revelations but as timely warnings and hopes for the broader world.

In these modern times, one might find it challenging to reconcile such mystic visions with the empirical reality we often hold dear. However, the essence of St. Faustina's experiences serves as a bridge between the tangible and the intangible, urging the faithful to live lives rooted in spiritual awareness. Her vivid descriptions of Jesus' merciful love and the outcome of moral choices provide a clarion call for introspection and transformation.

St. Faustina's impact is evident not just in her written "Diary" but also in the lasting devotion to Divine Mercy. Each year, Divine Mercy Sunday is celebrated on the Sunday after Easter, an occasion for the faithful to seek forgiveness and extend mercy to others. It's a day inspired by her visions, offering a profound opportunity for renewal and a reminder of God's boundless love.

In conclusion, St. Faustina's visions serve multiple purposes: they are a solemn warning, a beacon of hope, and a profound testament to the divine mercy that awaits all who earnestly seek it. Her life and visions challenge us to look beyond mundane existence, urging us to consider the spiritual ramifications of our actions and embrace a life of mercy, repentance, and faith. This is not about scaring one into belief but inviting a deeper understanding of divine love and justice.

As you reflect on St. Faustina's visions, may they inspire you not only to ponder the afterlife but to live a life worthy of divine mercy, ever seeking forgiveness and offering love in a world so desperately in need of it.

Padre Pio's Insights are as profound as they are unsettling, making them an essential part of understanding the stakes of our spiritual journey. Born Francesco Forgione, Padre Pio's life was steeped in miraculous happenings and profound spirituality. However, what makes his teachings particularly gripping is their sharp focus on the afterlife, both the splendor of heaven and the horror of hell.

Padre Pio, a man who could read souls and bilocate, frequently spoke about the urgencies of repentance and the reality of hell. He didn't mince words, either. For him, the afterlife wasn't just a place; it was a stark reality waiting for those who strayed from the path of righteousness. He once remarked, "The sinner who goes to Confession with a hardened heart shall go to hell, not for the sin which he confesses, but for the hardness of his heart." Such utterances were not designed merely to instill fear but to spark genuine repentance.

Imagine walking into the confessional, burdened by your wrongdoings, only to be met with the piercing gaze of Padre Pio. Those who experienced this described it as both horrifying and liberating. He had an uncanny ability to see right through the pretensions we carry, right into the state of our souls. What he sought was not just acknowledgment of sins but a transformation of the heart. A common theme in his teachings was the idea of a 'spiritual reboot,' a complete and authentic remorse leading one closer to God.

The gripping nature of Padre Pio's insights also lies in their directness. He vividly described hell as a place of eternal torment, where souls are not merely punished but are in a state of perpetual suffering due to their rejection of God's love. Such descriptions were not designed to be causal horror stories but to wake people up to spiritual realities. In a world increasingly indifferent to sin, Padre Pio's words serve as a jarring reminder of the consequences of moral laxity.

Yet, despite the grimness of his visions of hell, Padre Pio offered a pathway out of this dark destiny. His insight into the sacrament of Confession was groundbreaking in its simplicity: true repentance can alter the course of one's soul. He emphasized that Confession should be more than a ritualistic recounting of sins; it should be a moment of genuine contrition, a heartfelt plea for God's mercy.

One of Padre Pio's most haunting insights was a vision he had of the souls in hell. He recounted seeing countless souls condemned to eternal damnation and hearing their cries, which he described as a cacophony of despair. These souls, he said, were in hell not merely because they sinned, but because they refused God's mercy. He posited that our earthly life offers innumerable opportunities for repentance and redemption, but these opportunities must be seized earnestly.

Moreover, Padre Pio didn't limit his insights to visions of hell. His reflections on purgatory were equally enlightening, offering a mixture of horror and hope. He viewed purgatory as a great mercy, a temporal purification that saves souls from eternal damnation. However, he warned that the purification process was not to be taken lightly. According to him, the fires of purgatory, while purifying, were unbearably painful but infinitely preferable to the eternal fires of hell. His purpose in sharing these insights? To encourage the faithful to aim for heaven through diligent spiritual practice and genuine repentance.

Delving deeper, one learns that Padre Pio's teachings also encompassed spiritual warfare. He spoke of a constant battle between good and evil, taking place not just in some ethereal realm but within each human soul. According to him, every action, thought, and decision contributes to this cosmic struggle. The stakes are high, and complacency is a dangerous vice. His own life serves as a testament to this struggle, marked by incessant attacks from demonic forces. Yet, he remained unwavering in his faith and commitment to God, serving as a beacon for those grappling with their own spiritual battles.

In another striking insight, Padre Pio delved into the subject of grace. He asserted that grace is an indispensable weapon in the fight against sin and evil. Yet, grace must be actively sought and safeguarded through prayer, the sacraments, and a life of virtue. Receiving grace, according to him, is not a passive act but an active engagement with God's will. He implored the faithful to draw near to God, not just in moments of desperation but as a daily, habitual practice. These insights act as both a warning and a roadmap, highlighting the peril of ignoring God's grace and the blessings of embracing it.

Padre Pio was also known for his intense devotion to the Holy Eucharist, which he regarded as the pinnacle of grace. His insights on the sacrament were both profound and convicting. He often said, "It would be easier for the earth to exist without the sun than without the Holy Sacrifice of the Mass." For him, the Eucharist was the lifeblood of the soul, an inexhaustible source of spiritual nourishment. Through this sacrament, he believed, the faithful could receive the strength to resist temptation and the grace to grow in holiness.

His relationship with the Blessed Virgin Mary was another cornerstone of his spirituality. Padre Pio saw her as a powerful intercessor, urging the faithful to seek her help in their struggles against sin and temptation. He often described her as a mother who tirelessly advocates for her children before God. His insights into Marian devotion are a call to embrace this powerful form of spiritual support, ensuring that we are never alone in our battles. He said, "Love Our Lady and make her loved; always recite the Rosary. May the Blessed Mother of God reign sovereign over your hearts," signifying her unparalleled role in the Christian journey.

In providing these glimpses into the afterlife, Padre Pio offered not just warnings but also profound hope. He underscored that the road to hell is paved with missed opportunities for repentance, but the path to heaven, though arduous, is lined with signs of God's enduring love and mercy. The horrors he described serve a dual purpose: to shock us into awareness and to beckon us towards a life of greater sanctity.

Finally, the richness of Padre Pio's insights cannot be overstated. They serve as both a mirror and a compass, reflecting the state of our souls and guiding us towards a life imbued with God's love and grace. The urgency of his teachings lies in their timeliness; the stakes of our spiritual journey are too high for complacency. By embracing his insights on hell, purgatory, and divine grace, we find a roadmap to navigate the perilous terrain of our earthly lives and ultimately, to secure our place in the heavenly kingdom.

In essence, Padre Pio's insights demand a response. They challenge us to review our lives, to confess our transgressions, and to realign ourselves with God's will. They are a clarion call to awaken from spiritual slumber, to recognize

Encouraging Sinners to Repent

As we traverse through the narratives of Purgatory and Hell, one cannot help but feel a compelling urgency to steer clear of the paths leading to such harrowing fates. Within these realms, the prophecies and mystic visions of saints serve not just as fantastical tales but as sobering warnings and vital lessons meant to guide us toward repentance. Repentance, after all, is the cornerstone of reclaiming one's soul from the abyss and redirecting it toward divine grace.

In our daily lives, we encounter innumerable temptations and moral challenges that beckon us to stray from God's light. Often, it is easy to succumb, whether through moments of weakness or extended periods of spiritual dormancy. It is within these precarious gaps that sin takes root, growing silently yet persistently. Yet, acknowledging our sinful nature is the first step to repentance. If saints like St. Mary Magdalene and St. Paul could make their way back to God, despite the gravest of sins, so can we.

The resonant power of stories and visions from saints like St. Faustina and Padre Pio cannot be overemphasized. When St. Faustina describes the Hell she was allowed to witness, a place of perpetual darkness and suffering where souls languish in despair, the reader is meant to feel a shiver down their spine. Not merely as a reaction but as a clarion call for introspection. Being confronted with the severe consequences of unrepented sins serves as an electrifying deterrent and a profound motivator to live a life pleasing to God.

Yet, fear alone won't sustain us on the path to righteousness. Comedy, as paradoxical as it sounds, also plays a role. Humor can be a catalyst for humility. It's humbling to laugh at our own follies, to admit that we're flawed beings in need of redemption, and to understand that, despite our sinful past, there's always hope for divine mercy. This blend of horror and humor, of sacred and secular, makes the teachings all the more relatable and hence, effective.

Imagine knaves who ignored the gravity of repentance caused only because they underestimated the gentleness of divine love. Christ's love is not fluffy sentimentality; it is fierce and consuming. Its very nature demands us to turn away from our wrongdoings and seek forgiveness. Encouraging sinners to repent thus involves painting a full picture—sobering lessons of Hell, reminders of Heaven's bliss, and the transformative power of genuine contrition.

Repentance is not solely a private affair but a communal one. The Church, with its sacraments of Reconciliation and Eucharist, provides a framework to renew our covenant with God. We confess not because we relish in guilt but because it's the path toward freedom. Sins that are confessed lose their power, and the soul once shackled by secrecy is liberated.

The beauty of repentance lies in its accessibility to all. No sin is too great to be forgiven, and no sinner too lost to be found. God's mercy is without bounds, and the sacraments are our earthly conduits to that divine grace. Engaging in Confession grants peace and restoring the tarnished relationship with God brings indescribable joy.

Consider the impact of modeling repentance in our communities. When one soul repents, it sends ripples throughout a family, a parish, even a society. Conversion stories of saints have historically ignited waves of spiritual revival. So too can our daily acts of humility, seeking forgiveness and granting it, inspire those around us to turn their hearts back to God.

It's vital to understand that repentance is not an end but a process—a lifelong commitment to conversion. Each act of repentance is an invitation to deepen our relationship with God, making us ever more receptive to His grace. Far from merely avoiding Hell, the goal of repentance is sanctity—the pursuit of holiness in our daily lives.

Imagine how different our world could be if more of us embraced repentance. Conflicts would diminish as we seek reconciliation, injustices would lessen as we strive for righteousness, and our communities would flourish under the mantle of divine love and mercy. In a world rife with discord and moral ambiguities, the clear call to repentance offers a beacon of hope and a path to real transformation.

Repentance is also deeply tied to our sense of purpose. When we turn away from sin and align ourselves with God's will, we rediscover our reason for being. We are created not for the mundane but for the divine, not for fleeting pleasures but for eternal joy. This reconnection to our divine purpose imbues our lives with meaning and direction, making every day an opportunity to renew our commitment to God's will.

As you ponder the lessons from Purgatory and Hell, remember that the road to Heaven is paved with acts of repentance. Each time we acknowledge our failures and seek to amend them, we inch closer to divine grace. It's a journey fraught with challenges, no doubt, but it is also one filled with boundless divine assistance. God does not abandon those who seek His mercy; instead, He uplifts them, transforming sinners into saints.

In the myriad challenges of modern life, encourage all to seek solace in the Sacrament of Reconciliation. Let the confessional booth become a place of refuge rather than dread. Approaching it with genuine remorse and a heartfelt resolve to change, one not only receives absolution but also the strength to avoid future sins.

Reflect, then, on what more authentic joy there is than the joy of a soul freed from the burden of sin. Imagine the lightness, the peace, the renewed purpose that follows genuine repentance. It's not a fleeting happiness but a lasting transformation, a soul set on a path to eternal life.

Encouraging sinners to repent is not about casting judgment but about offering a lifeline of hope— a return to the arms of a loving Father who waits for us with eager anticipation. Whether it's through the stark warnings from saintly visions or the reassuring teachings of Christ's endless mercy, repentance brings souls back to their rightful place in God's eternal plan. So let us embrace, encourage, and exemplify this beautiful act of turning back to God, for in it lies our ultimate salvation and joy.

Chapter 11: Wholesome Catholic Jokes

Pope John Paul II, blessed with a keen wit and a warm heart, once quipped that a priest must always be ready to laugh at himself, for who else would dare? His playful spirit is a testament to the power of humor in faith, and his anecdotes invite us to find joy in our journey. Take, for instance, the tale of St. Philip Neri, whose penchant for humor earned him the title of "The Humorous Saint." Known to perform light-hearted acts such as shaving off half his beard before preaching, he aimed to keep the congregation light-hearted. He believed that a soul joyful in the Lord would be less inclined toward sin. Humor, you see, isn't a distraction—it's a divine tool to uplift spirits, encourage positivity, and make the arduous path of righteousness a little smoother. Let's cherish these wholesome Catholic jokes, for in laughter, we find a reflection of God's own joy.

Lighthearted Stories and Humor

In those moments when the world feels weighty and the road to holiness appears steep, a touch of humor can be just the balm for the soul. Picture St. Lawrence, who even amidst the flames could muster a smile and quip, "Turn me over; I'm done on this side!" Such lighthearted recountings not only tickle our funny bones but also remind us that joy and faith walk hand in hand. Amidst the grand orchestration of divine plans, there's beauty in recognizing that our saints, popes, and everyday believers often found God's grace in the simplest, most humorous corners of life. So let's celebrate the gift of laughter in our journey, where a well-timed joke might spark a conversion or restore a weary heart to the path of righteousness. For laughter, when shared in faith, becomes a sacred echo of the joy that awaits us all in God's loving embrace.

Jokes from the Life of Pope John Paul II hold a unique place in our hearts, illustrating the remarkable blend of his spiritual depth and playful spirit. Behind the solemn responsibilities he bore as the Holy Father lay a man who believed in the power of laughter as a divine gift. John Paul II often said that "a good laugh is as valid as a prayer," and his life was a testament to this conviction. His humor was not frivolous but rooted in a profound sense of hope and joy, characteristics essential for anyone walking the strenuous path of faith.

Pope John Paul II was known for his quick wit, even in the face of adversity. Once, after a serious conversation about the weighty matters of the Church, a cardinal commented on how daunting his responsibilities must be. With a twinkle in his eye, John Paul II responded, "You should see what it's like from my side of the desk!" His ability to meet challenges with a smile didn't just lighten the mood; it served as a beacon of hope and resilience for Catholics worldwide.

Behind this jovial exterior was a man intently aware of life's struggles. During a visit to the United States, he addressed a gathering at a seminary. The young seminarians, curious and somewhat nervous, started asking him questions, one of which was painfully direct, "Holy Father, how do you handle criticism?" With a broad smile, he answered, "I pray for my critics... it's not easy being them!" The room erupted in laughter, but the lesson was clear: compassion and understanding can be found even amidst criticism.

Even during intense moments of his papacy, John Paul II found ways to inject humor. During an audience with a high-ranking government official, he was asked how he juggled the responsibilities of his immense role. He leaned in, almost conspiratorially, and said, "With prayer... and a little help from my friends." This remark wasn't just a throwaway line but a reflection of his deep-seated belief in the community and the power of collective faith.

Another instance showcases his inexhaustible humor and pastoral care. A young boy once approached him and hesitantly asked if he had ever sinned. Taking the boy's hand gently, the Pope whispered, "Only my guardian angel knows how many times I've said 'oops' instead of 'amen'." The boy, along with the gathered faithful, erupted in laughter. But beyond the joke, it was an admission of shared human frailty, making the pontiff more accessible and relatable.

One of the most endearing examples of his humor was when he visited a parish in Rome, known for its dedicated but somewhat lethargic clergy. "How many priests work here?" he asked the parish priest. "About half of them, Holy Father," came the hesitant reply. John Paul II chuckled and said, "Ah, at least it's better than the Curia!" The laughter was instant, breaking the ice and encouraging a more fervent dedication from the clergy in attendance.

But perhaps one of his best-known humorous anecdotes happened during his younger years as a priest. Invited to a dinner party, he was mistakenly pegged as a 'Mr. Wojtyla' and not recognized as Father Wojtyla. When the host finally realized his error, he apologized profusely. John Paul II simply said, "That's alright! Tonight, I'll just be Mr. Wojtyla enjoying a good meal." This humility and humor highlighted his profound ability to connect with people from all walks of life.

His humor was not confined to direct interactions. It also translated into his speeches and writings. In one Easter message, he remarked on the length of the Vatican gatherings, saying, "Some of you were worried this homily would never end. Well, rejoice! Because that is the joy of Easter – new beginnings and new endings." This clever use of humor softened his messages, making his profound teachings more digestible and relatable.

A touching moment of laughter came from within the Pope's family circle. When asked by relatives why he kept climbing mountains and skiing even after becoming a bishop, he joked, "If I don't ski, God will think I'm not grateful for the beautiful mountains He created." This quip revealed his joy and gratitude for life, communion with nature, and unwavering spiritual connection with God's creation.

John Paul II harnessed humor as a powerful tool to uplift spirits. During an audience with seminarians worrying about their future roles, he quipped, "Don't worry about being the best priest. Just be a happy priest." The laughter that followed transformed the atmosphere, cementing the idea that joy and happiness are integral to spiritual leadership.

During another international trip, a journalist asked him what he would do if he had a vacation. John Paul II smiled and said, "I'd visit you all." This response, though light-hearted, underscored his boundless love for humanity and his eternal shepherding spirit. His humor illustrated that he carried the weight of the world not with a burdened heart but with resilient joy.

Indeed, one of his final humorous public remarks was directed at a long-standing aide who commented on the Pope's seemingly eternal energy despite his age. "Holy Father, how do you do it?" to which he wittily responded, "The secret is in my Polish genes and the Holy Spirit's support team!" A poignant laugh that showed the depth of his enduring faith, even as he faced deteriorating health.

Jokes from the Life of Pope John Paul II are not just snippets of laughter but are pearls of wisdom wrapped in humor. Each jest, each funny remark, carried within it a nugget of spiritual insight. His humor wasn't just an escape but a method of pastoral care, encouraging the faithful to find joy even amidst suffering and to trust in God's plan with a light heart. Through his jokes, John Paul II demonstrated that faith, hope, and love could be woven with laughter, making spiritual perseverance not just possible but joyous.

Uplifting Anecdotes from Saints bring the heavenly glow of humor into the hallowed corridors of the church, reminding us that even the saints walked this earth with joviality and wit. Consider the life of St. Teresa of Avila, a mystic who, despite her profound spiritual experiences, had an unmistakable sense of humor. Once during a particularly rough journey, she fell into a muddy stream and exclaimed, 'If this is how You treat Your friends, no wonder You have so few!' Her lightheartedness, even in discomfort, reminds us that laughter can be a sanctifying balm during our struggles.

St. Philip Neri, known for his joyful spirit, saw humor as an essential part of spirituality. One day, when a young man came to him boasting of grand plans for becoming a priest, St. Philip advised him to take more practical, humble steps first. He humorously said, 'First, let us begin with a pair of breeches.' This simple jocular advice was a grounding message about humility and the importance of starting with small, manageable goals. His life exemplifies that merriment can lead one towards greater humility and spiritual growth.

Laughter became a sanctifying act when St. Francis of Assisi employed humor to humble the prideful. Known for his affectionate teasing, he once found a young brother quite preoccupied with his intellectual knowledge. St. Francis put a tin pot on his head and called him a bishop, emphasizing that all titles and intellectual prowess are meaningless if devoid of humility. This endearing jest underscored the importance of simplicity and brought a gentle, humorous admonition against arrogance.

St. Lawrence, a deacon and martyr, displayed incredible bravery and humor even at the moment of his martyrdom. As he was being roasted alive on a gridiron, he reportedly called out to his executioners, 'Turn me over; I'm done on this side.' St. Lawrence's wit in the face of death illustrates how humor can be a powerful expression of the Christian belief in the Resurrection and eternal life. His courage mixed with humor continues to inspire and uplift the faithful in times of trial.

Then there's the tale of St. Joseph Benedict Labre, who had an unusual sense of humility that often manifested in quirky behaviors. As a beggar saint, he used to call dogs his brothers and would often share his meager food with them. Once, when reprimanded for giving his bread to a dog, he simply smiled and said, 'The dog's need was greater.' His ability to find joy and humor in his austere life demonstrates that sanctity often lies in recognizing and embracing the absurdities of life.

On the contrary, St. Ignatius of Loyola offered an anecdote of divine irony. After dedicating his life to God and founding the Jesuit order, he found his healthiest exercise to be enduring strenuous bureaucratic disputes within the church he so loved. He often joked that God had kept him fit more through paperwork than physical penance. It's a reminder that God's ways are mysterious and sometimes humorously intricate.

Another enlightening story comes from the life of St. John Bosco. Known for his playful nature, he once used magic tricks to attract children to his Oratory. Once a young boy was crying because he had lost his hat. St. John, with a sleight of hand, pretended to pull the hat out of thin air, delighting and consoling the child. His clever use of humor and magic was not just for amusement; it was a tool to bring children closer to the faith, demonstrating how laughter can be a conduit for God's grace.

St. Teresa of Calcutta also shared a moment of humor reflective of her deep humility. When asked by an interviewer what kept her going amidst so much suffering, she responded with her trademark twinkle in her eye, 'Of course, it's not me. It's all Him—plain and simple.' Her simple jest carried profound truth, pointing always to God's omnipotence over her own abilities. This light-hearted humility served as a reminder of the joy found in selfless service.

And who could forget the serene humor of St. John Paul II? Known for breaking the protocol with his warm and often humorous interactions, he once joked, 'The Pope is a man who loves his shoes,' when asked about his humble old footwear. His approachable humor made the lofty office of the papacy relatable to millions, bridging the gap between the divine mission of the Church and the everyday lives of the faithful.

St. Therese of Lisieux, though young and cloistered, had a wit that sparkled through her letters and writings. One humorous account shares how she once set her heart on saving souls through little acts of love and sacrifice. She quipped in her famous 'Little Way' that she was too small to scale the great heights of faith like the saints before her, so she would simply stay close to Jesus, who would lift her up without effort. Her simple, cheerful wisdom continues to guide many towards holiness through the path of childlike trust and humor.

Lastly, consider the lesser-known yet equally humorous story from the life of Blessed Solanus Casey. He was known for his dry wit and never taking himself too seriously. When asked about his many blessings despite being a humble doorkeeper, he responded, 'My soul, what have you ever done to deserve paradise?' It was a gentle reminder that God's grace operates beyond our merits, often in the most unexpected and humorous ways.

These uplifting anecdotes serve not only as delightful interludes but as profound lessons wrapped in humor. The saints, in their sanctified wit, beckon us to find joy in our spiritual journey. They remind us that holiness is not a somber affair but a jubilant path filled with divine irony and blessed laughter. In their relatable humanness, they bring heaven a little closer, and in their humor, they reveal the joyous heart of God.

Encouraging Joy and Positivity

In our journey through faith, it's easy to get weighed down by the challenges and adversities we encounter. Yet, a cheerful heart lightens the load and brings us closer to God. Humor and joy are not antithetical to holiness; rather, they complement it. When we laugh, we share in the communal spirit that has long been a cornerstone of Catholic fellowship. Just look at the lighthearted stories of saints and popes, who often used humor to teach important lessons and uplift those around them.

Consider the life of Pope John Paul II, a man known for his wisdom and his wit. He once quipped to an audience of seminarians, "I don't get the golf joke until after the crowd stops laughing. So no, I won't be taking up golf anytime soon." This kind of humor is not just amusing; it disarms and brings people together. In the laughter, we find our common humanity and a shared joy that transcends the mundane struggles of daily life.

The saints, too, have shown us that joy can be found in the simplest acts and moments of divine encounter. St. Philip Neri, often called the "Apostle of Rome," was known for his playful spirit. He once shaved half his beard before an important event just to shock the overly serious. His message was clear: God delights in our joy. It's a reminder that sanctity and humor can co-exist, enriching our spiritual lives and making us more approachable and inviting to others.

Joy is a powerful tool in evangelization. When we exhibit genuine happiness and positivity, others are naturally drawn to us. They might wonder, "What is the source of their joy?" This curiosity can open doors to deeper conversations about faith and the love of God. It is said in Proverbs 17:22, "A cheerful heart is a good medicine, but a crushed spirit dries up the bones." Joyful Catholics can be walking testimonies of God's love and grace, making the faith attractive and accessible to others.

Humor also has a way of diffusing tension and dispelling fear. In moments of crisis or sorrow, a well-timed joke or a smile can bring comfort and hope. Remember the words of St. Teresa of Avila, "God save us from gloomy saints!" She implored her fellow believers to find joy in their service to God, arguing that a dour disposition could undermine the Gospel message. Joy and positivity, sprinkled with humor, enable us to witness to the faith in a way that is compelling and relatable.

One poignant story of joy in the face of adversity is that of St. Lawrence, a deacon during early Christianity who was martyrdom by being roasted. According to tradition, in the midst of his suffering, he joked with his tormentors, saying, "Turn me over; I am done on this side." This dark humor shows a man completely unafraid of death, fully trusting in the eternal joy that awaited him. His cheerful courage inspires us to approach our own struggles with a light heart, assured of God's ultimate victory.

The power of humor in fostering joy and positivity is also evident in community life. Parish events, gatherings, and celebrations often feature jokes and light-hearted moments that break the ice and bring people closer together. These occasions remind us that our faith journey is not a solitary endeavor but a communal one. We laugh, we share, and in doing so, we grow in our faith, strengthening the bonds that tie us together.

Encouraging children and youth to embrace joy and positivity is particularly important. In a world that often bombards young minds with negativity, our laughter and happiness serve as beacons of light. When teaching religious education, incorporating humor can make lessons more engaging and memorable. Children are more likely to carry the faith into adulthood when it has been associated with positive experiences and joyful memories.

Moreover, humor can act as a safeguard against the pride that sometimes comes with piety. When we are able to laugh at ourselves, we acknowledge our human frailty and remain humble. This humility is crucial in our spiritual journey, keeping us grounded and reminding us that we are all sinners in need of God's grace. The saints often laughed at themselves, finding delight in their imperfections, which only made their testimonies more genuine and compelling.

While the formal aspects of our faith—prayers, sacraments, liturgy—provide the structure of our spiritual lives, joy and humor infuse it with vitality and warmth. The balance of solemnity and joy mirrors the complexity of our spiritual lives, underscoring that divine and human experiences are not mutually exclusive but harmoniously intertwined. When we incorporate humor into our faith practices, we reflect the joyful and inclusive nature of God's love.

To incorporate joy and positivity into our lives, we should remember to practice gratitude. Gratitude naturally leads to joy because it opens our eyes to the blessings around us, no matter how small. Whether it's the beauty of the sunrise, a kind word from a friend, or even a humorous moment, recognizing these blessings fills our hearts with joy, which we can then share with others.

In closing, let's always strive to bring joy and positivity into our lives and the lives of those around us. By sharing wholesome Catholic jokes, joyful stories from the saints, and humorous anecdotes, we're not only lightening our own burdens but also helping to uplift the spirits of our brothers and sisters in Christ. This shared joy embodies and communicates the profound beauty of our faith, making it a living, breathing testament to God's boundless love and mercy.

Chapter 12: Motivating Others on the Path to Righteousness

In an age where darkness often masquerades as light, motivating others to walk steadfastly on the path of righteousness is both a noble and urgent calling. Imagine the ironies of Oscar Wilde, the wit of Mark Twain, and the profound insights of Chesterton interwoven into our quest for truth and faith. Equip yourself with laughter to pierce the shadows, motivation to ignite the lethargic, and a touch of horror to stir the complacent. Through personal testimonies of grace and redemption, and the unflinching commitment to evangelization, we invite others to taste the celestial sweetness of a life aligned with divine will. As we navigate the winding roads of human frailty, let's become beacons of hope, illuminating the path to eternal wisdom and unshakable faith. The challenge is real, the stakes are eternal, but armed with humor, inspiration, and an occasional frightful reality check, we can lead even the most wayward souls back to the heart of the Church.

Personal Testimonies

There's something undeniably electrifying about hearing personal testimonies that kindle the spirit and ignite fresh fervor in one's heart. Consider the tale of an ordinary parishioner who, mired in doubt and despair, encountered a transformative moment of grace that redirected their entire life toward the path of righteousness. The weight of their struggles becomes palpable, yet so does the awe of their Divine encounter. These stories aren't secondhand accounts; they're real narratives from contemporary believers and members of our own communities. It's in these raw, honest testimonies that we find both the humor of human folly and the chilling reality of sin's consequences, punctuated by the hope of redemption. Such firsthand accounts serve as a vivid reminder that the path to righteousness isn't a solitary journey; we're enveloped by a choir of voices, each proclaiming the unwavering mercy and love of God. Personal testimonies illustrate that no soul is too lost, no heart too hardened, to feel the transformative touch of God's grace.

Voices of the Faithful echo through the corridors of time, a chorus of testimonies that ignite the spirit and kindle the flame of faith. These voices, ordinary yet extraordinary, provide profound glimpses into how God continues to work in the lives of His people. Their stories are not just tales of miraculous interventions but chronicles of hope, endurance, and the transformational power of divine grace.

Imagine the quiet strength of a mother who never gave up on her wayward son, praying the Rosary daily with unwavering faith. Her relentless prayers were answered when her son, once lost to the darkness of addiction, found his way back to the light, crediting his transformation to his mother's fervent intercession. This mother's voice joins the chorus, her story resonating with the truth that no prayer is ever wasted, and every plea whispered in the quiet of one's heart reaches the ears of the Almighty.

The story of a businessman named Mark offers another voice. Mark had it all—wealth, status, and luxury—yet his soul was impoverished. His heart ached for something more, something that money could never buy. It wasn't until he attended a retreat, reluctantly dragged along by a friend, that he encountered the living Christ. During Eucharistic Adoration, an overwhelming sense of peace enveloped him, leading to a profound conversion. He left behind his life of hollow pursuits to serve underprivileged communities, becoming a living testament to the power of grace and the joy of finding true purpose in Christ.

The voices of the faithful often reveal themselves in the simplest acts of kindness. Consider the elderly woman who attends daily Mass, her face radiating the quiet joy of communion with God. She carries a small, well-worn prayer book, its pages dog-eared from years of use. After Mass, she visits the local hospital, offering the comfort of prayer and companionship to those who suffer. Her voice resounds not in grand gestures but in the steady fidelity of living out the Gospel in everyday life.

These voices aren't confined to the past. Modern-day miracles continue to astonish and inspire. Take the case of Emily, a young girl diagnosed with a terminal illness. Her family, staunch believers, turned to the intercession of St. Rita, the patroness of impossible causes. They prayed with fervor, never losing hope. Miraculously, Emily's condition began to improve, baffling doctors who could offer no medical explanation. Today, she stands as a living miracle, her life a testament to the enduring power of faith and prayer.

Then there's the story of Leo, a disillusioned former priest who had lost his way and left the Church. His life had been one of doubt and cynicism until he encountered an old friend, now a devout Catholic. Through patient dialogue and gentle witness, Leo was drawn back to the faith he had abandoned. Experiencing genuine contrition and receiving the Sacrament of Reconciliation, he felt rejuvenation unlike any other. His voice is a powerful reminder that it's never too late to return to God, no matter how far one might stray.

Even in the face of adversity, the voices of the faithful refuse to be silenced. Let's recall the plight of Maria, a single mother facing the bleakest of financial situations. With mounting bills and little means, she turned to her parish community for help. In a remarkable display of the Body of Christ in action, the community rallied around her, offering not just monetary assistance but emotional and spiritual support. She weathered the storm with the help of her faith and her community, her voice a proclamation of the strength found in unity and faith.

The voices of the faithful also resound in the lives of modern mystics who, through divine encounters, remind us that the mystical realm is not a relic of the past. Consider John, an average man who began experiencing visions after a near-death experience. His visions, rich with symbolism and prophetic insight, led him to embark on a mission of evangelization, drawing many back to the Church. John's voice, initially hesitant and uncertain, grew strong and compelling, a beacon for those searching for meaning and truth.

Faith perseveres against the darkness, resonating through those who offer their lives in sacrifice. Think of Ann, a nurse who contracted a severe illness while caring for COVID-19 patients. Her decision to continue working, despite the risks, stemmed from a deep conviction in her call to serve. Though she eventually succumbed to the illness, her dedication and faith left an indelible mark on her community. Ann's voice, though now silent, speaks volumes about the depth of love and the courage born of faith.

Finally, we turn our attention to the many martyrs of faith, those who have given their lives for the name of Christ. Their voices transcend time, offering the ultimate witness to the truth of the Gospel. Take the example of young Luis, a seminarian during a time of religious persecution. Despite the threat of torture and execution, he refused to renounce his faith. His final moments were spent reciting the Lord's Prayer, his voice unwavering even in the face of death. Luis serves as a powerful reminder that faith, even unto death, holds the victory.

In conclusion, the "Voices of the Faithful" encapsulate the essence of a living Church, one that is continually renewed through the witness of its members. These voices reach across the centuries, binding us together in a tapestry of divine intervention, miraculous conversions, and enduring faith. They inspire us, challenge us, and call us to a deeper relationship with God. Through their stories, we find strength, hope, and the assurance that God is ever-present, guiding us on the path to righteousness.

Modern Miracles and Divine Encounters draw us into a realm where the ordinary meets the extraordinary, where faith transforms into tangible signs from the heavens. These modern marvels serve as a testament to God's unceasing presence in our lives, even amidst the din of modernity. They defy the skeptical glances and whispered doubts, revealing a reality steeped in divine mystery and love.

Consider the bleeding statues, the icons that weep, and the Eucharistic hosts that transform mysteriously. In a church in Buenos Aires, a host bled, drawing national attention and even scientific scrutiny. DNA tests stressed us beyond comprehension, for the blood examined seemed to bear traits of heart tissue, perplexing scientists and skeptics alike. These elements call us to a deeper reflection—to see beyond the surface and to embrace the miracles as invitations to deepen our faith.

One cannot forget the heart-wrenching story of a young girl from Mexico, who suffered an inoperable tumor. Her parents, worn and yet unwavering in their faith, took her to a shrine dedicated to Our Lady of Guadalupe. There, amidst fervent prayers and tear-streaked faces, the tumor disappeared. Medical experts were at a loss, offering no rational explanation. For the believers, however, it was clear: a divine hand had intervened, a gentle reminder that miracles do happen.

Delve into the annals of recent history, and the account of Audrey Santo of Worcester, Massachusetts, emerges. Audrey, an innocent child who entered a coma after a swimming pool accident, became a conduit for miraculous phenomena. Oil exuding from her statues, stigmata appearing on her body, and inexplicable healings attributed to her prayers—all these point to a world where the spiritual interweaves seamlessly with the physical.

In Italy, the case of Natuzza Evolo offers an unsettling yet profoundly moving glimpse into spirit-filled life. An ordinary woman blessed with extraordinary gifts, Natuzza bore the marks of Christ's Passion, experienced regular conversations with saints, and had sustained mystical phenomena all her life. Her story compels us to confront our own assumptions, to open our hearts to the inexplicable, and, perhaps most importantly, to engage more deeply with our faith.

Then there's the tale of a humble farmer from India who experienced a divine encounter that's left a mark on his village forever. Caught in a moment of despair, he claimed to have seen St. Thomas the Apostle, who directed him to dig at a particular spot. There, he uncovered an ancient relic of St. Thomas himself. The relic now resides in a new church, built to mark the miracle, bringing pilgrims from far and wide.

Also worthy of attention is the phenomenon of Marian apparitions that continue to grace our times. Despite initial skepticism, sites like Medjugorje in Bosnia and Herzegovina have attracted millions, reporting miraculous healings and spiritual awakenings. Some might consider these visions as mere flights of pious fancy, yet the myriad testimonials and physical transformations witnessed speak volumes.

Moreover, the synchronistic and mind-boggling occurrence known as "the Miracle of the Sun," witnessed by thousands at Fátima, echoes into modern times. Similar experiences have been reported recently, albeit on a smaller scale. Such events defy logical explanation and invite us to marvel at the manifold mysteries God reveals to us, often in broad daylight and clear view.

Let's not overlook the stories closer to our own lives, the everyday miracles that often go unnoticed. A priest in a small parish recounts how a family, struggling with their faith, lit candles, prayed fervently, and witnessed as their wayward son returned home after years of separation. You may call this a coincidence, but for those who live in faith, it's an answered prayer, a modern-day miracle that serves to renew and invigorate their spiritual journey.

These modern miracles and divine encounters present themselves not just as displays of divine power but as moments of grace, opening our hearts to deeper faith and commitment. They remind us that, amidst the noise and chaos of contemporary life, God's grace reaches us, often in unexpected and awe-inspiring ways. Their impact is quietly profound, leaving ripples across our spiritual landscape.

Miracles aren't relics of the past; they are woven into the very fabric of our existence, echoing the ageless truths of our faith. Their awe and wonder remind us that the divine is never far. In an age of skepticism, these blessings serve as anchors of hope and beacons of God's enduring love.

In a world where science often reigns supreme, these encounters challenge our understanding and beckon us towards mystery. They invite us to step beyond the empirical and to embrace a spiritual truth that transcends the limits of human knowledge. They ignite in us a sense of humility and awe, renewing our fervor and conviction in the omnipotent and omnipresent God.

Whether through grand, public spectacles or the quiet, intimate corners of our lives, modern miracles and divine encounters reach into our hearts, refreshing our spirits and reaffirming our unwavering faith. They whisper to us of a reality far greater than our own, encouraging us to hold steadfast in our spiritual journey, to continue praying, seeking, and believing.

The Importance of Evangelization

Evangelization, dear reader, is often misunderstood as a mere missionary journey to distant lands, far removed from our everyday lives. However, it's much more nuanced and essential to the fabric of Roman Catholic life. Evangelization isn't just about converting others; it's about igniting a spark of faith that spreads like wildfire, driven by hope, love, and sometimes a tinge of divine comedy. It's the art of motivation wrapped in divine wisdom, straightforward and complex all at once, like a holy paradox.

Imagine a world where every Catholic took evangelization to heart, embedding it into their daily actions. The transformative power would be immeasurable, for evangelization at its core is a ripple effect initiated by the quiet acts of individuals. It's not just about preaching from the pulpit but living a life that becomes a testament to the teachings of Christ. You don't need to go door-to-door with a Bible in hand; sometimes, it's about how you live, how you love, and how you persevere amid life's trials.

In our journey on the path to righteousness, the pivotal role of evangelization cannot be overstated. Every saint, every mystic, every visionary we revere today was once a spark set alight by someone else's act of faith. Let us not forget that St. Paul, one of the greatest evangelizers, began as the most fervent persecutor of Christians. It was his dramatic conversion, influenced by an encounter with Jesus, that sparked the evangelical fire that spread across continents.

What Church history teaches us is that evangelization is an ongoing, communal effort. Think of it as a symphony where every instrument plays a part. You might be a violin adding delicate harmony or a booming drum making the ground shake—each contribution is vital. Through acts of charity, conversations filled with grace, and a living example of Christ's teachings, we evangelize. This collaborative effort underlines the importance of unified faith, a testament to the strength of community in the Catholic Church.

It's crucial to embrace this mission with humility and humor. Let's inject a bit of lightheartedness into our faith journey, for even the most potent lessons can be delivered with a twinkle in the eye and a well-timed joke. After all, wasn't it G.K. Chesterton who said, "Angels can fly because they take themselves lightly"? Remember, evangelizing should never feel like a heavy burden but a joyous sharing of the most profound gift we possess.

However, let's not shy away from the horror that sometimes accompanies the absence of evangelization. In the shadows where light hasn't been cast, darkness festers. Souls are lost, despair takes root, and the path to righteousness becomes overgrown with thorns. By neglecting evangelization, we allow these shadows to grow. Yet, the inverse is gloriously true: by evangelizing, we shine the light that scatters this darkness. We become beacons guiding others out of the abyss and onto the path illuminated by our Lord.

In every moment and interaction, there's an opportunity to evangelize. A smile to a stranger, a kind word to a co-worker, or even a simple "God bless you" can be the spark that fans into a flame of faith. In today's digital age, we have even more tools at our disposal for this sacred mission. Social media posts, blogs, and online discussions can be avenues for sharing the gospel. Done thoughtfully, these modern platforms can be extensions of our evangelistic mission.

Consider St. Francis of Assisi, who said, "Preach the Gospel at all times. When necessary, use words." His life was a brilliant tapestry of quiet evangelization through service, compassion, and unwavering faith. It's a gentle yet powerful reminder that actions often speak louder than words. The love we show, the kindness we offer, are the most effective sermons we can deliver.

Yet, the task isn't always easy. Sometimes, it requires courage and resilience. We may encounter skepticism, resistance, or even hostility. When this happens, remember the stories of saints and martyrs who faced far worse yet stood firm in their conviction. Every challenge you face in evangelizing strengthens your faith and ability to lead others to righteousness. It's a cyclical growth—a relationship with God that deepens as you help others discover Him.

But let's not forget the laughter along the way. Humor can be a powerful evangelistic tool. A well-timed jest can disarm the skeptical, open hearts, and build bridges where there were once walls. The history of the Church is replete with saints who used humor to break down barriers and bring people closer to God. St. Philip Neri, known as the "humorous saint," made faith accessible and engaging through his wit.

Ultimately, the importance of evangelization lies in its ability to renew the Church, invigorate the faithful, and pave the way for sinners to find redemption. It's a living, breathing testament to God's love and mercy. Every time we evangelize, we tell the world that the path to righteousness is not a solitary journey but a communal pilgrimage,

filled with laughter, tears, triumphs, and
trials.

So embrace evangelization with the spirit of
a poet, the courage of a soldier, and the
heart of a shepherd. Relish in the joy of
sharing your faith and witnessing its
transformative power in others' lives. Let
your life be a testament to the teachings of
Christ, a living sermon that inspires,
motivates, and, most importantly, leads
others on the path to righteousness and
wisdom. After all, what could be more
beautiful, more fulfilling, than partaking in
the divine mission of leading souls to God?

Conclusion

As we draw our journey to its close, it's clear that faith is the symphony of the soul. It's not simply a series of rituals or rote recitations. It's a love story, a comedy, and sometimes even a thrilling horror tale, all rolled into one. We've walked through the riveting pages of miracles, saints, exorcists, and visionaries, and our faith should now be set ablaze with renewed fervor and inexhaustible hope.

Consider for a moment the saints whose lives we've explored. They were not born superhuman. They faced struggles, doubts, and immense challenges, yet they remained unwavering in their faith. St. Francis of Assisi, with his profound love for all of God's creatures, and St. Therese of Lisieux, who found the sublime in small acts of love, serve as perfect canvases upon which we can inscribe our own aspirations for holiness. If they could, why can't we?

Then there are the mystics and visionaries who gave us glimpses into realms beyond our mortal coil. Such experiences are more than just tales to marvel at; they are divine whispers urging us to mend our ways. The haunting visions of Purgatory and Hell shared by saints like St. Catherine of Genoa and Blessed Anne Catherine Emmerich aren't meant to terrify us into submission, but to inspire genuine repentance and a heart open to God's mercy.

One can't ignore the intense and often terrifying confrontations from the world of exorcism. These aren't subjects conjured in the minds of Hollywood scriptwriters, but real, bone-chilling encounters that remind us of the lurking evil and, more importantly, the overwhelming power of God. The stories of exorcists and their struggles against malevolent forces serve as potent symbols of spiritual warfare, urging us to be vigilant and steadfast in our own battles.

Remember the pearls of wisdom from the saints—aphorisms and teachings that have weathered the test of time. St. Augustine's introspective insights and St. Teresa of Avila's mystical teachings offer us guideposts along our spiritual path. These teachings, distilled through centuries of holy wisdom, can steer us away from life's pitfalls and lead us toward true fulfillment.

Repentance isn't just a relic of the past but a transformative power available today. The poignant stories of conversion, like those of St. Paul and St. Mary Magdalene, remind us that no one is beyond redemption. Their stories are encouraging beacons guiding us towards our own spiritual renewal. Embrace repentance in your daily life, not as a burden, but as a liberating act that draws you closer to God's loving embrace.

We've seen how living a fulfilling spiritual life is both a privilege and a discipline. Daily practices such as prayer, meditation, attending Mass, and receiving the Sacraments aren't mere obligations but sacred encounters with the Divine. These habits build a fortress around our faith, safeguarding us against the volatile storms of modern life.

Acts of love and charity bring the Gospel to life in ways that words alone cannot. The legacies of icons like St. Vincent de Paul and Mother Teresa are testaments to the miraculous impact of simple, heartfelt actions. Modern examples of Catholic charity continue to echo their noble mission, compelling us to love and serve with similar zeal.

Hope is the lifeline that keeps our spirit buoyant amidst life's tempests. The stories of St. Monica and St. Jude, along with countless others, show us that hope isn't a mere sentiment but a resilient force rooted in faith. When the shadows of despair encroach, it's hope that lights our way, ensuring that we never lose sight of God's enduring promises.

Purgatory and Hell, though daunting, are realities whispered to us through the visions and warnings of saints like St. Faustina and Padre Pio. Their insights beckon us to strive for holiness and encourage us to lead others away from the path of perdition. Eternal consequences loom, and they must catalyze our conversion and earnest life of virtue.

And let's not forget the joy that humor can bring. The wholesome Catholic jokes sprinkled throughout this journey remind us that laughter is indeed a gift from God. Whether it's a lighthearted story from Pope John Paul II's life or an uplifting anecdote from the saints, humor can be a healing balm, fostering community, and reminding us of life's lighter side.

Lastly, motivating others on the path to righteousness is our collective calling. Personal testimonies and evangelization efforts underscore the profound impact of sharing our faith narratives. Whether it's recounting modern miracles or divine encounters, our stories can serve as catalysts for conversions and deepen the faith of those who might be wavering.

This conclusion isn't an end but a new beginning. It's a call to arms, a gentle whisper urging you to keep fighting the good fight, to keep loving, serving, praying, and hoping. May your faith become a beacon for others, guiding them towards the joy, peace, and eternal life promised by our loving

Creator. Let courage and conviction fuel your steps, for the road to righteousness is demanding but beautifully rewarding.

Appendix A: Appendix

Welcome to the final section of our journey together. In this appendix, you'll find a treasure trove of resources aimed at nurturing your faith, offering solace, and providing the tools necessary to deepen your spiritual walk. Whether you're just beginning your journey or have been traversing this path for years, these resources are meant to support you every step of the way.

Prayers and Devotions

Prayer is the lifeline of faith. It connects us to the Divine and strengthens our spirit. This section offers a collection of traditional Catholic prayers and devotions that have been the bedrock of countless saints and believers throughout history. From daily prayers to specific devotions, these words can serve as your guide in seeking comfort, wisdom, and divine intervention.

- **The Our Father:** The quintessential prayer taught by Jesus Himself.

- **The Hail Mary**: A beautiful invocation seeking the Blessed Mother's intercession.

- **The Rosary**: A meditative journey through the mysteries of Christ's life.

- **The Divine Mercy Chaplet**: A powerful prayer given to St. Faustina, emphasizing trust in God's boundless mercy.

Resources for Further Reading

The quest for spiritual enlightenment doesn't end with the final page of this book. For those who thirst for more wisdom, we've curated a list of invaluable resources that delve deeper into the themes discussed herein. These books, articles, and websites are authored by spiritual heavyweights and learned theologians, offering fresh perspectives and deeper insights.

1. **The Catechism of the Catholic Church**: An indispensable resource

for understanding the doctrines and teachings of the Church.

2. **The Lives of the Saints**: Various compilations that provide inspiring biographies of holy men and women.

3. **The Confessions of St. Augustine**: A timeless spiritual autobiography that explores conversion and grace.

4. **Online Resources**: Vatican.va, NewAdvent.org, and Catholic.com offer a wealth of articles and documents to explore.

Contact Information for Prayer Groups and Support

Community is crucial in the spiritual journey. Connecting with others who share your faith can provide encouragement, accountability, and fellowship. Below, you'll find some avenues to connect with prayer groups and support networks that can walk alongside you in your spiritual journey.

- **Local Parish Groups**: Most Catholic parishes offer various groups and ministries. Reach out to your parish office for more information.

- **Online Prayer Forums**: Websites and forums like the "Catholic Answers Forum" and "Prayer Warriors" offer online communities where you can share intentions and receive prayer support.

- **National Catholic Organizations**: Organizations like the Knights of Columbus, the Catholic Women's League, and others have chapters nationwide and offer both spiritual and social opportunities.

Remember, the path to righteousness and wisdom is both personal and communal. Utilize these resources to enrich your faith, seek comfort in times of trial, and connect with the broader body of Christ. Here's to your continued growth in faith, hope, and love. Go forth and live the Gospel with joy, courage, and unwavering conviction.

Prayers and Devotions

Prayer, dear friends, is not a mere ritual but the breath of the soul, a lifeline connecting us to the Divine. It's easy to dismiss these moments of calm, murmurs of fervent pleas, and thankfulness as routine, yet within them lies a potent force that has shaped history, changed lives, and moved God's heart. Devotion, on the other hand, embodies a sacred rhythm of life, a dedication that transcends mere obligation and blooms into a profound relationship with our Creator.

Imagine the early morning mist lifting as faithful arise, their lips whispering "Our Father" with eyes still heavy from sleep. The "Hail Mary," sung by countless generations, echoes through the ages, an undying serenade to the Mother of God. These aren't just words, but bridges built from the Earth to Heaven.

Intertwined with these prayers are the devotions that color our spiritual landscape. The Rosary, that chain of Our Lady's Roses, guides us through the precious mysteries of Christ's life. Each bead, a step closer to understanding His sacrifice, His love, and His mercy. The Divine Mercy Chaplet invokes His boundless compassion at the three o'clock hour, a time made holy by His death. Let's not forget the Angelus, a daily pause to remember the Incarnation, the moment God entered our world in flesh and humility.

Pouring over the pages of a prayer book, with hands clasped tightly, one finds solace in centuries-old devotions. From the litanies invoking saints' intercession to novenas seeking specific graces, the multitude of prayers sustains us in our daily crosses. Consider the Litany of Humility, a formidable entreaty for the humbling of our egos. Or the Novena to the Holy Spirit, where we implore for the gifts that ignite our faith and courage.

In the silence of a chapel, the Adoration of the Blessed Sacrament draws the faithful to their knees, quiet yet profoundly expressive. Here, amidst the soft flicker of candles, the faithful encounter the Real Presence – a mystery so grand that words fall short. Engaging in Eucharistic Adoration allows for a sacred dialogue where words are often replaced by the eloquence of silence, and hearts speak directly to Christ.

Consider also the rich heritage of Marian devotions. Society may shift and values evolve, yet the fervent love for the Blessed Mother endures unwaveringly. May devotions, crowned by the annual May crowning, embody a communal tribute to her queenship. The Scapular of Our Lady of Mount Carmel, a simple cloth, yet a profound pledge of protection, serves as a reminder of her maternal care.

But dear pilgrim, there is more. Ever-struggling souls find respite in the Stations of the Cross, a walk through Christ's Passion, reliving His suffering step by step. As each station unveils, we're drawn into the heart of His sacrifice, compelled to reflect on our own burdens and how inadequate they seem in comparison.

Moving beyond the personal, look at the collective power of prayer. When communities gather, their unified voices resonate louder, lifting urgent petitions Heavenward. The beauty of the Liturgy of the Hours emanates from its persistent rhythm, casting prayers like lifelines at fixed hours, creating an unending cascade of devotion.

Yet, let's not sidestep the more intense forms of prayer and devotion. The prayers of exorcism stand as stark reminders of the spiritual warfare that pervades our existence. These aren't for the faint-hearted but are crucial, invoking the power of Christ to dispel the darkness. The Rite of Exorcism, steeped in the Church's authority, affirms the presence of evil but emphasizes God's prevailing power.

Amidst devotion is also the blend of sacrifice, seen in fasting and abstinence, acts that purify and strengthen the spirit. Lenten practices, days of penance, and the discipline of abstaining from comforts, mirror Christ's own sacrifices. They're not about mere deprivation but about creating a void that God Himself fills.

The prayers of the saints are treasures of our tradition. The St. Michael Prayer shields against nefarious forces, while the Prayer of St. Francis transforms hearts towards peace and love. St. Patrick's Breastplate, both a hymn and a prayer, is an armor of faith, invoking the Blessed Trinity's protection.

As you navigate through these prayers and devotions, remember that each one was born out of a deep yearning to touch the Divine. They are timeless, adaptable to every era, resonating with the same fervor today as they did centuries ago. They are schools of virtue, teaching patience, humility, and resilience.

Let us not overlook the many saints whose devotions have transformed lives. Think of St. Teresa of Avila and her contemplative prayers that draw souls into intimate union with God, or St. Ignatius of Loyola's Examen, a nightly reflection to discern God's presence in our daily activities. These devotions, while unique in their expression, all lead to the same end—closeness with God.

And so, dear wanderer in faith, immerse yourself in this tapestry of prayers and devotions. They are your roadmap amidst the world's chaos, your comfort in distress, and your companions in solitude. They remind you that in every whisper, sigh, and plea, you're partaking in a celestial conversation, joining an eternal chorus that reaches the very heart of God.

Resources for Further Reading

As we delve into the appendix of our spiritual journey, it's important to recognize that one can never have enough resources to galvanize faith, bolster knowledge, and inspire righteous living. This section provides further recommendations for books, articles, and websites that will give you the tools to explore your faith more deeply. These resources span a vast range of topics, offering insights from theology to practical guidance for everyday spiritual living.

First, consider looking into *Summa Theologica* by St. Thomas Aquinas. This work is a treasure trove of theological insights that delve into almost every aspect of faith and reason. Aquinas's logical arguments, although written centuries ago, remain profoundly relevant and can help deepen your understanding of not only Catholic doctrine but also the interconnectedness of faith and rational thought.

For those interested in diving into the compelling lives and wisdom of the saints, Butler's *Lives of the Saints* provides detailed biographies and spiritually enriching narratives. These stories illustrate the heroic virtues and extraordinary faith of saints who have gone before us, serving as timeless models for living a devout Catholic life. You'll find that the trials and triumphs of these holy individuals often mirror our own struggles, guiding us towards finding strength and solace in our faith.

Pope John Paul II's rich literary contributions cannot be ignored. His encyclicals, especially *Fides et Ratio* (Faith and Reason), provide profound expositions on the harmonious relationship between faith and intellectual inquiry. His personal reflections in *Crossing the Threshold of Hope* offer an intimate look into the mind of one of the most influential leaders of the modern Catholic Church.

If you're searching for works that emphasize sinners' conversion and the transformative power of repentance, consider St. Augustine's *Confessions*. This autobiographical work presents a gripping narrative of personal transformation that transcends time, making it a powerful read for anyone seeking redemption and a deeper relationship with God.

Another treasure is the *Diary of St. Faustina Kowalska*. Often called the "Apostle of Divine Mercy," St. Faustina's diary captures her mystical experiences and conversations with Jesus Christ. It highlights God's infinite mercy and love for humanity, providing a source of comfort and encouragement for those struggling with sin and despair.

Turning to modern writers, Scott Hahn's *Rome Sweet Home* offers a contemporary journey of conversion and discovery. His engaging narrative recounts his transition from Protestantism to Catholicism, punctuated with humor, drama, and profound theological insights. It's an excellent resource for those wrestling with questions of faith or contemplating conversion.

For a deep dive into Marian apparitions and their significance, *The Woman Clothed with the Sun* by John J. Delaney is a must-read. It details various apparitions of the Blessed Virgin Mary and their implications for the Catholic faith. The stories not only inspire but also remind us of Mary's enduring presence and influence within the Church.

Additionally, the works of G.K. Chesterton, especially *Orthodoxy* and *The Everlasting Man*, offer a delightful blend of wit and profound wisdom. Chesterton's ability to articulate complex theological ideas in an accessible and often humorous manner makes his books a joy to read.

If you prefer more structured spiritual exercises, St. Ignatius of Loyola's *Spiritual Exercises* offers a structured guide to meditative prayer and reflection. These exercises are designed to deepen one's spiritual life and foster a closer relationship with God. They are particularly useful for retreat settings or personal spiritual renewal.

Then there is *Mere Christianity* by C.S. Lewis, which, although not exclusively Catholic, provides compelling arguments for basic Christian beliefs that resonate deeply with Catholic teaching. His lucid prose and logical clarity can help bridge gaps in understanding and reinforce your journey to faith.

For those grappling with darker spiritual battles, Malachi Martin's *Hostage to the Devil* offers chilling yet enlightening exorcism accounts. Though not for the faint-hearted, this book underscores the reality of spiritual warfare and the power of God's deliverance in the face of evil. It's a sobering reminder of the necessity of prayer and vigilance in our spiritual lives.

Theological encyclopedias such as *The Catholic Encyclopedia* are invaluable for those who seek concise and authoritative explanations on a myriad of topics within the Catholic faith. It's a handy reference for deepening your understanding of complex doctrines and historical developments.

Moreover, online platforms like the Vatican's official website (www.vatican.va) offer a wealth of resources, including papal encyclicals, Church documents, and news relevant to the global Catholic community. It serves as a digital repository of crucial texts and contemporary discussions, making it an indispensable tool for ongoing faith formation.

Lastly, consider subscribing to renowned Catholic periodicals like *The Catholic Herald* and *First Things*. These publications offer a blend of in-depth articles, current events, and thoughtful reflections that can keep you informed and inspired in your faith journey.

In summary, this list is but the tip of the iceberg. Each resource opens a new avenue for exploration, inviting you to delve deeper into your Catholic faith. The lives of the saints, the prayers of the devout, the wisdom of theologians, and the divine revelations all serve to illuminate the path toward righteousness and wisdom. Whether you seek solace, inspiration, or knowledge, these readings promise to enrich your spiritual life and guide you closer to God.

As you continue on your faith journey, remember that you're not alone. Draw strength from the community of believers, both past and present, and never hesitate to seek guidance and inspiration from these invaluable resources. May they imbue your spirit with hope, courage, and unwavering faith.

Contact Information for Prayer Groups and Support

At times, the journey of faith can feel akin to a solitary walk through a dense, bewildering forest—a place where clarity eludes you and each step forward conjures new uncertainties. Yet, it's in this very wilderness that a melodious, reassuring chorus beckons, guiding us back to the light. This soulful melody emanates from the countless prayer groups and support networks that punctuate the Catholic community. Whether you are dealing with personal struggles, spiritual unrest, or seeking communal worship, these groups are your sanctuary.

The simplest way to start is to connect with your local parish. The church bulletin, often a humble, unassuming pamphlet, is a treasure trove of information. It lists various prayer groups, study sessions, and support gatherings that cater to a myriad of spiritual needs. Consider, for example, the Rosary prayer groups, a staple in many parishes. These devoted congregations gather to recite the Rosary, offering prayers for peace, protection, and divine intercession. The power of collective prayer shouldn't be underestimated; it's like a veritable shield against the adversities that besiege our souls.

On the practical side, contact your parish office for specific details, such as meeting times and locations. Most parishes are more than eager to help newcomers integrate into their supportive communities. The office staff, often dedicated volunteers themselves, can also connect you with spiritual directors for personal guidance.

If the traditional route feels mundane, fear not! The digital age offers a plethora of resources. Various websites and online forums offer directories of prayer groups. For instance, the Catholic Online Directory (catholic.org) allows you to search for groups based on locality and specific needs. The United States Conference of Catholic Bishops (usccb.org) also provides a plethora of resources, including links to national and international prayer groups and support networks.

For those who appreciate the intimacy of smaller gatherings, look no further than lay-led support groups. These networks, often founded by individuals who've undergone transformative experiences, offer a more personal touch. One shining example is the Legion of Mary, an apostolic organization grounded in prayer and active engagement in the community. Their meetings, rich in camaraderie and devotion, are a haven for anyone seeking both spiritual and emotional support.

Meanwhile, charismatic prayer groups can provide a different flavor of spiritual encounter. Known for their enthusiastic worship and spontaneous prayer, these groups pursue a vibrant, kinetic form of devotion. They meet regularly in church basements, homes, and community centers, bringing life to neighborhoods with their effusive spirituality. Again, checking with your parish office or bulletin can guide you to these groups.

Beyond local community connections, there exists a tapestry of national and international organizations dedicated to prayer and support. Consider, for instance, the Society of St. Vincent de Paul. Not merely a charitable organization, it acts as a bridge, connecting those in need with volunteers ready to offer both spiritual and material help.

Then, there are the Knights of Columbus, whose very existence is synonymous with support and fraternity. Their chapters abound in parishes globally, providing not just opportunities for prayer and service, but for meaningful brotherhood. Most importantly, they are just a call or an email away, making them accessible even in the most remote corners of the world.

Don't overlook the transformative power of social media, either. Platforms like Facebook and Twitter host numerous Catholic groups focused on prayer and support. By searching for groups related to your interests or struggles, you can join vibrant online communities that, despite the distance, offer warmth and solidarity. These digital enclaves often feature regular live prayer sessions, discussions, and encouragement from fellow believers.

Let's not forget the dedicated prayer lines available for those in immediate need of spiritual support. These hotlines, often staffed by compassionate volunteers, provide a confidential space for prayer and guidance. Organizations such as the EWTN Prayer Line (1-800-447-3986) or the Upper Room Living Prayer Center (1-800-251-2468) stand as testaments to our faith's commitment to supporting one another.

Another remarkable resource is the platform established by the Apostleship of Prayer, known today as the Pope's Worldwide Prayer Network (popesprayer.va). This initiative not only facilitates global prayer intentions but also offers an app (Click to Pray) to unite faithful from every corner of the globe in real-time, communal prayer.

In more specific needs, there are retreats and specialized support groups that address particular issues such as addiction, grief, or family matters. For instance, Rachel's Vineyard is an extraordinary retreat program designed for healing after abortion. Similarly, GriefShare and other Christian-based support groups provide solace to those navigating loss.

Your diocesan website is another gateway to exploring these options. Most dioceses have comprehensive lists of local and national support groups, retreats, and prayer communities. This can be especially helpful in finding specialized support tailored to your personal journey.

Finally, nothing beats the power of word-of-mouth in our faith communities. Speak to your priest, deacon, or fellow parishioners. Ask for recommendations during confession or spiritual direction sessions. You might be surprised by the networks hidden in plain sight, ready to envelope you in their loving support.

In essence, the flip side to the isolation you might feel on a perilous spiritual journey is the unimaginable network of support awaiting your discovery. The collaboration of devoted souls within prayer groups and support networks is nothing less than awe-inspiring. They are the unsung heroes of our faith, standing in the gap, lifting each other up, and ensuring no one walks the path of faith alone.

So venture forward confidently, knowing that whether through a parish pamphlet, a digital directory, or the sympathetic ear of a fellow believer, a myriad of prayer groups and support networks await to guide, uplift, and unite us in our common pursuit of divine grace.

THE 15 PRAYERS OF ST. BRIDGET

These Prayers and these Promises have been copied from a book printed in Toulouse in 1740 and published by the P. Adrien Parvilliers of the Company of Jesus, Apostolic Missionary of the Holy Land, with approbation, permission and recommendation to distribute them.
Pope Pius IX took cognisance of these Prayers with the prologue; he approved them May 31, 1862, recognising them as true and for the good of souls.

As St. Bridget for a long time wanted to know the number of blows Our Lord received during His Passion, He one day appeared to her and said: "I received 5480 blows on My Body. If you wish to honour them in some way, say 15 Our

Fathers and 15 Hail Marys with the following Prayers (which He taught her) for a whole year. When the year is up, you will have honoured each one of My Wounds."

He made the following promises to anyone who recited these Prayers for a whole year:

1. I will deliver 15 souls of his lineage from Purgatory.
2. 15 souls of his lineage will be confirmed and preserved in grace.
3. 15 sinners of his lineage will be converted.
4. Whoever recites these Prayers will attain the first degree of perfection.
5. 15 days before his death I will give him My Precious Body in order that he may escape eternal starvation; I will give him My Precious Blood to drink lest he thirst eternally.
6. 15 days before his death he will feel a deep contrition for all his sins and will have a perfect knowledge of them.
7. I will place before him the sign of My Victorious Cross for his help and defence against the attacks of his enemies.
8. Before his death I shall come with My Dearest Beloved Mother.
9. I shall graciously receive his soul, and will lead it into eternal joys.
10. And having led it there I shall give him a special draught from the fountain of My Deity, something I will not for those who have not recited My Prayers.
11. Let it be known that whoever may have been living in a state of mortal sin for 30 years, but who will recite devoutly, or have the intention to recite these Prayers, the Lord will forgive him all his sins.
12. I shall protect him from strong temptations.
13. I shall preserve and guard his 5 senses.

14. I shall preserve him from a sudden death.
15. His soul will be delivered from eternal death.
16. He will obtain all he asks for from God and the Blessed Virgin.
17. If he has lived all his life doing his own will and he is to die the next day, his life will be prolonged.
18. Every time one recites these Prayers he gains 100 days indulgence.
19. He is assured of being joined to the supreme Choir of Angels.
20. Whoever teaches these Prayers to another, will have continuous joy and merit which will endure eternally.
21. There where these Prayers are being said or will be said in the future God is present with His grace.

Each prayer is preceded by one Our Father and one Hail Mary.

Our Father, who art in heaven, hallowed be thy name.
Thy kingdom come.
Thy will be done on earth as it is in heaven.
Give us this day our daily bread and forgive us our
trespasses as we forgive those who trespass against us and
lead us not into temptation but deliver us from evil. **Amen**

Hail Mary, full of grace, the Lord is with thee; blessed art
thou among women and blessed is the fruit of thy womb,
Jesus.
Holy Mary, Mother of God, pray for us sinners, now and at
the hour of our death. **Amen.**

FIRST PRAYER
Our Father - Hail Mary.
O Jesus Christ! Eternal Sweetness to those who love Thee,
joy surpassing all joy and all desire, Salvation and Hope of
all sinners, Who hast proved that Thou hast no greater
desire than to be among men, even assuming human nature

at the fullness of time for the love of men, recall all the sufferings Thou hast endured from the instant of Thy conception, and especially during Thy Passion, as it was decreed and ordained from all eternity in the Divine plan.

Remember, O Lord, that during the Last Supper with Thy disciples, having washed their feet, Thou gavest them Thy Most Precious Body and Blood, and while at the same time thou didst sweetly console them, Thou didst foretell them Thy coming Passion.
Remember the sadness and bitterness which Thou didst experience in Thy Soul as Thou Thyself bore witness saying: "My Soul is sorrowful even unto death."

Remember all the fear, anguish and pain that Thou didst suffer in Thy delicate Body before the torment of the Crucifixion, when, after having prayed three times, bathed in a sweat of blood, Thou wast betrayed by Judas, Thy disciple, arrested by the people of a nation Thou hadst chosen and elevated, accused by false witnesses, unjustly judged by three judges during the flower of Thy youth and during the solemn Paschal season.

Remember that Thou wast despoiled of Thy garments and clothed in those of derision; that Thy Face and Eyes were veiled, that Thou wast buffeted, crowned with thorns, a reed placed in Thy Hands, that Thou was crushed with blows and overwhelmed with affronts and outrages.
In memory of all these pains and sufferings which Thou didst endure before Thy Passion on the Cross, grant me before my death true contrition, a sincere and entire confession, worthy satisfaction and the remission of all my sins. **Amen.**

SECOND PRAYER
Our Father – Hail Mary.
O Jesus! True liberty of angels, Paradise of delights, remember the horror and sadness which Thou didst endure

when Thy enemies, like furious lions, surrounded Thee, and by thousands of insults, spits, blows, lacerations and other unheard-of-cruelties, tormented Thee at will.

In consideration of these torments and insulting words, I beseech Thee, O my Saviour, to deliver me from all my enemies, visible and invisible, and to bring me, under Thy protection, to the perfection of eternal salvation. **Amen.**

THIRD PRAYER
Our Father – Hail Mary.
O Jesus! Creator of Heaven and earth Whom nothing can encompass or limit, Thou Who dost enfold and hold all under Thy Loving power, remember the very bitter pain.

Thou didst suffer when the Jews nailed Thy Sacred Hands and Feet to the Cross by blow after blow with big blunt nails, and not finding Thee in a pitiable enough state to satisfy their rage, they enlarged Thy Wounds, and added pain to pain, and with indescribable cruelty stretched Thy Body on the Cross, pulled Thee from all sides, thus dislocating Thy Limbs.

I beg of Thee, O Jesus, by the memory of this most Loving suffering of the Cross, to grant me the grace to fear Thee and to Love Thee. **Amen.**

FOURTH PRAYER
Our Father – Hail Mary.
O Jesus! Heavenly Physician, raised aloft on the Cross to heal our wounds with Thine, remember the bruises which Thou didst suffer and the weakness of all Thy Members which were distended to such a degree that never was there pain like unto Thine.

From the crown of Thy Head to the Soles of Thy Feet there

was not one spot on Thy Body that was not in torment, and yet, forgetting all Thy sufferings, Thou didst not cease to pray to Thy Heavenly Father for Thy enemies, saying: "Father forgive them for they know not what they do."

Through this great Mercy, and in memory of this suffering, grant that the remembrance of Thy Most Bitter Passion may effect in us a perfect contrition and the remission of all our sins. **Amen**.

FIFTH PRAYER
Our Father - Hail Mary.
O Jesus! Mirror of eternal splendour, remember the sadness which Thou experienced, when contemplating in the light of Thy Divinity the predestination of those who would be saved by the merits of Thy Sacred Passion.

Thou didst see at the same time, the great multitude of reprobates who would be damned for their sins, and Thou didst complain bitterly of those hopeless lost and unfortunate sinners.

Through this abyss of compassion and pity, and especially through the goodness which Thou displayed to the good thief when Thou saidst to him: "This day, thou shalt be with Me in Paradise." I beg of Thee, O Sweet Jesus, that at the hour of my death, Thou wilt show me mercy. **Amen**.

SIXTH PRAYER
Our Father - Hail Mary.
O Jesus! Beloved and most desirable King, remember the grief Thou didst suffer, when naked and like a common criminal.

Thou was fastened and raised on the Cross, when all Thy relatives and friends abandoned Thee, except Thy Beloved

Mother, who remained close to Thee during Thy agony and whom Thou didst entrust to Thy faithful disciple when Thou saidst to Mary: "Woman, behold thy son!" and to St. John: "Son, behold thy Mother!"

I beg of Thee O my Saviour, by the sword of sorrow which pierced the soul of Thy holy Mother, to have compassion on me in all my affliction and tribulations, both corporal and spiritual, and to assist me in all my trials, and especially at the hour of my death. **Amen**.

SEVENTH PRAYER
Our Father - Hail Mary.
O Jesus! Inexhaustible Fountain of compassion, Who by a profound gesture of Love, said from the Cross: "I thirst!" suffered from the thirst for the salvation of the human race.

I beg of Thee O my Saviour, to inflame in our hearts the desire to tend toward perfection in all our acts; and to extinguish in us the concupiscence of the flesh and the ardor of worldly desires. **Amen**.

EIGHTH PRAYER
Our Father - Hail Mary.
O Jesus! Sweetness of hearts, delight of the spirit, by the bitterness of the vinegar and gall which Thou didst taste on the Cross for Love of us, grant us the grace to receive worthily.

Thy Precious Body and Blood during our life and at the hour of our death, that they may serve as a remedy and consolation for our souls. **Amen.**

NINTH PRAYER
Our Father - Hail Mary.

O Jesus! Royal virtue, joy of the mind, recall the pain Thou didst endure when, plunged in an ocean of bitterness at the approach of death, insulted, outraged by the Jews.

Thou didst cry out in a loud voice that Thou was abandoned by Thy Father, saying: "My God, My God, why hast Thou forsaken me?"

Through this anguish, I beg of Thee, O my Saviour, not to abandon me in the terrors and pains of my death. **Amen.**

TENTH PRAYER
Our Father - Hail Mary.
O Jesus! Who art the beginning and end of all things, life and virtue, remembers that for our sakes Thou was plunged in an abyss of suffering from the soles of Thy Feet to the crown of Thy Head.

In consideration of the enormity of Thy Wounds, teach me to keep, through pure love, Thy Commandments, whose way is wide and easy for those who love Thee. **Amen.**

ELEVENTH PRAYER
Our Father - Hail Mary.
O Jesus! Deep abyss of mercy, I beg of Thee, in memory of Thy Wounds which penetrated to the very marrow of Thy Bones and to the depth of Thy being, to draw me, a miserable sinner, overwhelmed by my offenses, away from sin and to hide me from Thy Face justly irritated against me, hide me in Thy wounds, until Thy anger and just indignation shall have passed away. **Amen.**

TWELFTH PRAYER
Our Father - Hail Mary.
O Jesus! Mirror of Truth, symbol of unity, bond of charity,

remember the multitude of wounds with which Thou wast afflicted from head to foot, torn and reddened by the spilling of Thy adorable Blood. O great and universal pain, which Thou didst suffer in Thy virginal flesh for love of us! Sweetest Jesus! What is there that Thou couldst have done for us which Thou has not done!

May the fruit of Thy suffering be renewed in my soul by the faithful remembrance of Thy Passion, and may Thy love increase in my heart each day, until I see Thee in eternity: Thou Who art the treasure of every real good and every joy, which I beg Thee to grant me, O Sweetest Jesus, in heaven. **Amen.**

THIRTEENTH PRAYER
Our Father - Hail Mary.
O Jesus! Strong Lion, Immortal and Invincible King, remember the pain which Thou didst endure when all Thy strength, both moral and physical, was entirely exhausted, Thou didst bow Thy Head, saying: "It is consummated!"

Through this anguish and grief, I beg of Thee Lord Jesus, to have mercy on me at the hour of my death when my mind will be greatly troubled and my soul will be in anguish. **Amen.**

FOURTEENTH PRAYER
Our Father - Hail Mary.
O Jesus! Only Son of the Father, Splendour and Figure of His Substance, remember the simple and humble recommendation.

Thou didst make of Thy Soul to Thy Eternal Father, saying: "Father, into Thy Hands I commend My Spirit!" And with Thy Body all torn, and Thy Heart Broken, and the bowels of Thy Mercy open to redeem us, Thou didst Expire.

By this Precious Death, I beg of Thee O King of Saints, comfort me and help me to resist the devil, the flesh and the world, so that being dead to the world I may live for Thee alone.

I beg of Thee at the hour of my death to receive me, a pilgrim and an exile returning to Thee. **Amen.**

FIFTEENTH PRAYER
Our Father – Hail Mary.
O Jesus! True and fruitful Vine! Remember the abundant outpouring of Blood which Thou didst so generously shed from Thy Sacred Body as juice from grapes in a wine press.

From Thy Side, pierced with a lance by a soldier, blood and water issued forth until there was not left in Thy Body a single drop, and finally, like a bundle of myrrh lifted to the top of the Cross Thy delicate Flesh was destroyed, the very Substance of Thy Body withered, and the Marrow of Thy Bones dried up.

Through this bitter Passion and through the outpouring of Thy Precious Blood, I beg of Thee, O Sweet Jesus, to receive my soul when I am in my death agony. **Amen.**

CONCLUSION
O Sweet Jesus! Pierce my heart so that my tears of penitence and love will be my bread day and night; may I be converted entirely to Thee, may my heart be Thy perpetual habitation, may my conversation be pleasing to Thee, and may the end of my life be so praiseworthy that I may merit Heaven and there with Thy saints, praise Thee forever. **Amen.**

www.ingramcontent.com/pod-product-compliance
Lightning Source LLC
Chambersburg PA
CBHW071921150726
47999CB00001B/62